WATCH OUT

Here comes Lewis Grizzard, the man who jolted hypochondriacs with *They Tore Out My Heart and Stomped That Sucker Flat*, the three-time loser who blew the whistle on marriage in *If Love Were Oil, I'd Be About a Quart Low*, the worldly philosopher of *Elvis is Dead and I Don't Feel So Good Myself*.

Now, in *Don't Sit Under the Grits Tree*, America's hottest new humorist

... clarifies the Moral Majority position on chewing gum

... explains the difference between "naked" and "nekkid" (One means having no clothes on, the other means having no clothes on and you're up to something)

... and gives a frank opinion on Bra Padders, Preppies, "The Love Boat" and people who say "Grizzard" like it rhymes with "gizzard."

"Few American humorists can reach down and pull so much out of themselves as Lewis Grizzard."

—*Atlanta Journal-Constitution*

"Imagine Andy Rooney with a Georgian accent . . . and a sense of humor."

—*Houston Post*

Also by Lewis Grizzard

Elvis Is Dead, and I Don't Feel So Good Myself
If Love Were Oil, I'd Be About a Quart Low
Kathy Sue Loudermilk, I Love You
They Tore Out My Heart and Stomped that Sucker Flat
Won't You Come Home, Billy Bob Bailey?

Published by
WARNER BOOKS

Don't Sit Under The Grits Tree With Anyone Else But Me

Lewis Grizzard

Warner Books, Inc.
1271 Avenue of the Americas
New York, N.Y. 10020

A Time Warner Company

Printed in the United States of America
First Warner Books Printing: 1982

Reprinted: January, 1994

A Time Warner Company

WARNER BOOKS EDITION

Copyright © 1981 by Lewis Grizzard
All rights reserved.

This Warner Books Edition is published by arrangement with Peachtree Publishers Limited, 494 Armour Circle, N.E., Atlanta, Georgia 30324.

Warner Books, Inc.
1271 Avenue of the Americas
New York, N.Y. 10020

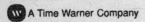 A Time Warner Company

Printed in the United States of America

First Warner Books Printing: June, 1985

Reissued: January, 1989

10 9

To
Helen Elliott
who believes in angels.

CONTENTS

1 SOCIAL STUDIES

2 CORDIE MAE AND THE GANG

5 EATING LIVER AND OTHER SINS

6 A THIRD LOOK AT LOVE AND MARRIAGE

7 CATS AND DOGS

8 SPECIAL OCCASIONS

9 ELECTION YEAR

10 NUMBER ONE

11 PEACH OF A STATE

1

SOCIAL STUDIES

If you hang out around salad bars, work in a bank, have a cute name like "Traci," speak a foreign language, are a professional athlete who says, "Hi, Mom" when you're on television, are overweight, slurp your soup, jog, are a lardbutt, wear padded bras, or don't like old-fashioned soda fountains, maybe you'd better pass up Chapter One and go directly to Chapter Two . . . .

Take This Salad Bar and Shove It

It finally happened to me the other night at dinner in a restaurant. First, the waiter brought water and bread, and then the menu.

After taking my order, he said, "You may help yourself to our salad bar."

It had been some time coming, but the band of restraint inside me finally snapped.

"I DON'T WANT TO HELP MYSELF TO YOUR SALAD BAR!" I screamed.

"SALAD BARS DRIVE ME INSANE!" I continued, my eyes rolling back in my head.

"I think he's speaking in tongues," a woman said to her husband in the booth next to mine.

"Shut up, Gladys," said the man. "He's just high on a jalapeno pepper."

"YOU CAN TAKE YOUR STUPID SALAD

3

BAR AND SHOVE IT!" I went on, now completely out of control.

The waiter, in complete shock, fetched the restaurant manager, who calmed me with buttered saltines.

I have been foursquare against the idea of salad bars since they first reared their ugly lettuced heads in American restaurants.

It is a matter of principle with me.

Whenever I go out to a restaurant, and pay good money, I expect the following:

● Good food.

● No loud music or pinball machines in the area where you actually eat.

● To be waited on hand and foot.

If I want to go to the trouble of preparing my own salad, I will do it in the privacy of my own home, where I can eat it in my underdrawers if I so desire.

"But," salad-bar types are always arguing with me, "with a salad bar, you can put exactly what you want, and how much you want of it, on your salad."

I can get the same thing and never move one inch from my seat.

"Waiter, what do you have available for salads in this establishment?"

"Sir, we have lettuce, tomatoes, cucumbers, mushrooms, radishes, peppers, onions, bacon bits, and Italian, Thousand Island, French, and Groovy Garlic dressings."

"I'll have a heaping serving of everything but

4

the radishes (radishes taste like a ping-pong ball would probably taste if it were solid), heavy on the Groovy Garlic dressing."

I sit there while my waiter, who is a trained professional in this sort of thing, prepares my salad.

Frankly, it is difficult to find my sort of restaurant these days, one that doesn't dispense its salads from a salad bar. Even the fast-food chains have come over:

Welcome to El Flasho's Taco Take-Out: Mi Salad Bar Es Su Salad Bar."

Soon, I expect all sorts of other establishments, even those that aren't normally associated with food, to get involved.

"Bubba's Transmission Shop: If We Can't Fix It, It Ain't Broke, Visit Our Salad Bar."

Or, "Henning, Henning, Henning, Watts and Schmedlap, Attorneys at Law. Featuring the Best Salad Bar in Town."

I simply can't understand the appeal of making your own salad in a restaurant. If you think that's fun, try something really dynamite like grinding up your own hamburger.

Which probably is the next fad in American restaurants. You stop off on the way to the restaurant and pick up a few pounds of hamburger, potatoes, and salad mixings.

At the restaurant they show you into the kitchen, where you cook your own dinner, and then you serve your own table. Afterwards, you get to clean your table, and then wash your dishes and mop. Hot water is extra.

And will the last customer to leave please remember to turn off the lights?

All Quiet in the Bank

I often have wondered why more people don't suffer nervous breakdowns when they go into banks. Each time I go into a bank, I emerge with sweaty palms and a pounding heartbeat.

That is because each time I go into a bank, I become so frustrated that I want to rant and rave and scream, but it always is so *quiet* in a bank, which is something else that frustrates me.

Why should people be quiet in a bank? I can understand being quiet in a library or in a funeral home, or even in a doctor's office because there are sick people around, but what's the big deal about keeping your voice down in a stupid bank?

What could they do to you if you suddenly started making a lot of noise while standing in line waiting for a teller?

Is an officer of the bank going to come out from behind one of those wooden doors with the brass nameplates and say, "I'm sorry, sir, but you will have to deposit your money in another financial institution if you can't learn to be quiet while you are in our bank"?

Of course not. Banks just have conned us into thinking they are some kind of big deal where you have to whisper and wear deodorant like when you're in a fancy-smancy restaurant.

Standing in line in a bank is just like standing in line at the grocery store waiting to buy tomatoes. You can chat and sing and even make sucking noises through your teeth and they're still going to sell you those tomatoes because they want their greedy hands on your money.

Next time you're in a bank, break into "The Star Spangled Banner" and I promise nobody will do a thing, except that maybe a few people in your line will think you're nuts and leave the bank, and then you will be able to get to the teller more quickly.

That's something else that drives me crazy about banks. When they build banks, they always build a lot of teller windows. I bank at a small bank. There are maybe ten teller windows at my bank.

Never in the history of my bank have there been more than five tellers behind windows at one time, and three of them always have "Next Window Please" signs keeping customers away while the line stretches out the front door.

If there are ten teller windows, why can't there be ten tellers? Where ARE the other tellers? Probably back in the vault being beaten for making an effort to hurry through transactions with less than fifty people waiting in the line.

But let me tell you what REALLY cracks me up about banks. Their pens. The ones that are chained to the penholders that are nailed to the desks where you are supposed to fill out your deposit slips.

Every time I go into my bank, it's the same with those pens. I go to the first desk and one of the penholders is empty because somebody has ripped off the pen.

So I pick up a second pen, but it doesn't work. I shake it, rub it across the paper a couple of times, and shake it again. Still, it doesn't work.

I go to the second desk. Same problem. Either the pens have been lifted or they don't work.

Why, I have complained, can't a bank maintain a couple of pens that work? And how can I trust a bank to keep my money safe when it can't even keep an eye on a couple of crummy pens?

But nothing ever changes. The next time I go into my bank, the pen situation will be the same, there still will be two tellers for ten windows, the line will be long and you would think somebody just had died the way everybody is being so careful to whisper.

If I had the guts, I would start making sucking noises through my teeth and fill out my deposit slip with a pink crayon.

"T" is for "Traci"

Lisa, who is in the second grade, was sending out Christmas cards to her girlfriends at school the other evening.

"How do you spell 'Shannon'?" she asked me.

I told her.

"And how do you spell 'Tracy'?" she went on.

I told her that, too. Only it turned out I was wrong. Nobody spells "Tracy" like that anymore. Now, they spell "Tracy" like this: T-r-a-c-i.

Names are like anything else. They come and they go. What has happened since I was a kid is we've had a complete turnover in the sort of names people give to their children.

What the present generation of parents is doing is naming their children "cute" names, like "Shannon" and "Traci" and "Debi" and "Marti" and "Pipsie" and "Amy."

For boys, names like "Sean" are big these days, along with "Chad," "Trey," "Geoff," and "Biff," which is what people used to name their dogs.

Don't get me wrong. I think people can name their kids anything they want. The man for whom the Lear Jet is named, for instance, put "Shanda" on his daughter.

But there are some great names that appear to have been all but forgotten.

When was the last time you heard of a kid

named Clarence, for instance? Good name, "Clarence."

Or how about a "Thelma"? There was even a song about a Thelma:

> *"T" for Texas,*
> *"T" for Tennessee,*
> *"T" for Thelma,*
> *Woman made a fool out of me.*

Imagine bringing out the same emotion with " 'T' for 'Traci.' "

I went to school with a lot of Arnolds. In fact, one of the craziest people I have ever known was named Arnold. Arnold Davenport.

It was in the second grade, I think, when Arnold Davenport found a worm on the playground and ate it. You have to be crazy to eat a worm.

And how many children do you know named Marvin these days? Be careful of anybody named Marvin, too. I went to school with Marvin Millingham, who distinguished himself by allowing a cherry bomb to explode in his hand to show his girlfriend, Imogene Norsworthy, how much courage he had.

Marvin's mother wanted him to be a concert pianist, but so much for that. Imogene Norsworthy, meanwhile, wasn't impressed and started going with Arnold Davenport.

Being from the South, I was used to double names. The possibilities were endless:

BOYS: Billy Bob, Billy Joe, Billy Frank, Bob Billy, Joe Billy, Frank Billy, Jim Bob, Joe Bob, Joe Frank, Willie Joe, Joe Willie, Bobby Earl, Henry Lee, Lee Roy, and one of my all-time favorites, Jack Joe Jenkins, who later married Imogene Norsworthy and moved to Johnson City.

GIRLS: Betty Joe, Bobbie Jo, Jo Jo, Jessie Jo, Jessie Jewell, Jo Beth, Sophie Joe, Sophie Mae, Cordie Mae, Hattie Mae, Linda Lou, Lisa Lou, Betty Lou, Betty Lou Ann Sue, and Kathy Sue Loudermilk, who made Imogene Norsworthy look like a sack of sweet potatoes.

As for me, I was named for my father. His name was Lewis, too. Once, I asked my mother what they would have named me if I had been a girl.

"Same thing," said my mother. "Your father would have insisted."

Thank the Lord it never came to that. Imagine a girl going through life with a name like "Lewis." Some things are worse than eating a worm.

Language Snobs

Most Americans have no interest in learning about language. Learning how to speak English good is hard enough.

There was this one kid from my hometown who went off to the big university and took a lot of French courses. When he got home, he went all over town bragging he had become bilingual.

His entire family was shamed, and the Methodist minister prayed for his retrieval from the deviates who had led him into such a depraved state.

In other countries it is nothing for mere schoolchildren to speak several languages. In high school I took two years of Spanish, but they made me do it.

I hated Spanish. Two years of Spanish, and here is my entire Spanish vocabulary:

> *Si.*
>
> *El beisbol es un juego de Mexico y Norte America, tambien.*
>
> *Ricardo Montalban.*
>
> *Del Taco.*
>
> *Pepe Frias.*

Pepe Frias, incidentally, plays *beisbol* for the Los Angeles Dodgers. He plays like he just had a bad batch of tacos.

What prompted me to think about all this was a report from the U.S. Embassy in Afghanistan. In case you missed it, a Russian soldier fighting in that country recently sought refuge in the U.S. Embassy.

But there was a big problem. None of the Americans at the U.S. Embassy could interrogate the soldier because none of the Americans spoke any Russian, and the Russian didn't speak any English.

Think about that. About a zillion Russian soldiers came marching across the border in Afghanistan months and months ago, and we still don't even have anybody there who would know what the devil they were talking about if he overheard Russian generals discussing whose border they were going to cross next.

I think the big problem is Americans are snooty when it comes to other languages. Why should WE learn their language? Let THEM learn ours.

That attitude is one of the reasons that when you go to France these days, and a waiter finds out you are an American, he deliberately spills hot coffee in your lap, and if there's not already a fly in your soup, he'll find one.

The point is, the State Department is stupid for not having somebody who speaks Russian in our embassy in Afghanistan, and I just remembered another story that happened in my hometown. It involves a French exchange student and Claude (Goat) Rainwater, who worked at the local service station.

Goat Rainwater had never been outside the county. But he did watch a little television, and he made the tenth grade before he quit school.

Once the church sponsored a French student to come to live in various homes for the summer. The idea was that maybe some of her culture—and language—would rub off on the rest of us.

The first day she was in town, we took her—Michelle—to meet Goat Rainwater.

"Goat, this is Michelle," one of the group said. "She's from France."

"Wellll," replied Goat, realizing this wasn't your everyday, garden variety drop-in at the service station. "*Como esta usted, Senyoreetar?*"

Nobody bothered to correct him, and instead of Michelle teaching us any French, we taught her to cuss like an American sailor who has just been rolled in a bar on the dark side of Tijuana.

Hi, Mom

I have watched a lot of football games on television this year. In some ways, football is a lot better on television than it is in person.

The rest rooms are not as far away when you watch the game on television, for instance.

What else is great about watching the game on the tube is you get to see the players close up. Sometimes they will even show taped interviews of the players while the action is slow on the field.

"While the action is slow on the field, let's show you an interview with Dallas linebacker Eldo (Mad Dog) Rado taped before the game."

"Eldo, what are Dallas's chances of getting into the Super Bowl this season?"

"Well, you know, if we, you know, can, you know, win, you know, a, you know, couple of, you know, more, you know, games this, you know, season, then, you know, we, you know, got a, you know, pretty good, you know, uh, chance, you know."

It doesn't say anywhere in the standard NFL contract that a player must be able to play pass defense and handle the English language at the same time.

What has become a silly practice on televised games, however, is focusing a camera on players while they are on the sidelines, drinking Gatorade, spitting, or eating some of the astroturf.

It is human nature to attempt to perform, or say something clever, when you go one-on-one with a television camera.

But all football players say the same thing in that situation.

They say, "Hi, Mom."

If I have seen one football player say, "Hi, Mom," to a television camera this season, I have seen a thousand.

What is this, "Hi Mom?" Football players make tons of money. Why don't they pop for a long distance call occasionally and say, "Hi, Mom," then, instead of using up precious time on network television that costs the average sponsor millions?

I would like for a football player to think of

something original occasionally when he is before the camera.

"Hi, Dad" would do for starters.

Or, "I would like to take this opportunity to thank both my parents for making me eat the right foods and get my rest so that I would grow strong and tall and be able to come out here on Sunday afternoons and tear my opponents limb from limb."

And why stick to relatives?

"Hi, Bettyann, I know I said I would call, but, golly, the big game was coming up and we had practice all week, and I got this bad case of jock itch, and then I got drunk and lost my playbook, and that girl who answered the phone at my apartment when you called the other night was my cousin from Shreveport who's a nun."

Or why not try to say something intelligent or meaningful to the audience?

"Remember, my fellow Americans, that the game of life is a lot like football. You have to tackle your problems, block your fears, and score your points when you get the opportunities; otherwise, some bad dude like Mean Joe Coca-Cola is gonna come along and stomp your head right into the ground."

The only player who never says, "Hi, Mom" when he is on camera, as a matter of fact, is Dallas' Eldo (Mad Dog) Rado. That's because he doesn't have a mother. They grew him in a forest in northern California, you know.

Abundant Americans

We have studies for practically everything today—studies to see why frogs leap and why rabbits hop and why birds don't fly upside down.

One of my favorite studies lately was the one about fat people. A group in Maryland studied fat people and concluded they are being discriminated against almost as much as blacks and "other minorities."

I didn't know that. See why we have to grant all those tax funds to have studies?

David Tucker, the consultant who directed the study for the Maryland Human Relations Commission, said fat people are victims of discrimination in nearly every aspect of life.

He said fat people have trouble getting jobs because employers don't want them in contact with the public.

He said employers tend to characterize fat people as "lazy, lacking in self-discipline, not well-motivated, sloppy, unclean, and, in one case, smelly."

He said owners of theaters and sports arenas don't make their seats wide enough for fat people, and he probably should also have mentioned airplane seats, because I know a fat person who has to buy two seats every time he flies. If the arm rests won't go down, he straddles them.

We do discriminate against fat people, don't we?

17

We poke fun at them. There was a guy I knew in college. He was fat as a pig. That's why we called him "Hog-Body"—Hog-Body Spradlin.

I never did know Hog-Body's real name until years later when I ran into him at a cocktail party and he was wearing a name tag. His real name was Norbert, which explains why he never complained when we called him Hog-Body.

We especially poke fun and discriminate against fat women. You never see fat women doing pantyhose commercials or selling shampoo on television.

The first question out of any man's mouth as soon as a blind date has been arranged for him is, "She isn't a fat girl, is she?"

That comes immediately after he has been told she makes her own clothes and "all the girls like her."

I think it was Alex Karras, former football player, broadcaster, and some-time actor, who said the worst thing I have ever heard said to a fat girl.

It supposedly happened at a dance when Alex Karras was a student at Iowa. He was in the clutches of a rather large young woman, but, being the nice fellow that he is, he wanted to pay her a compliment.

He came up with the classic, "You don't sweat much for a fat girl."

Alex Karras is no nice fellow. He is a cad.

We also bicker at fat people about going on diets.

My friend Ludlow Porch, an Atlanta radio announcer, isn't exactly slender. ("The local Little League team," he is fond of saying, "gets in shape by running a few laps around me.")

He hates to go to the doctor because he doesn't want to be told to go on a diet again.

"I went to see the doctor the other day," he was telling me. "He said, 'Ludlow, you're overweight.'"

"I said, 'I know that, doctor, and you're short. I can lose weight, but what are you going to do about your situation?'"

My idea is that we lay off fat people. No more discrimination, no more cute remarks. We could even cut the word "fat" out of our vocabularies.

Instead of saying "fat people," let's say "abundant Americans." "Roly-poly" and "plump" and "rotund" and "obese" and "porky" are words no member of polite society should dare say from now on.

In fact, the only time "fat" should really be accepted is when it refers to a body of our government handing out a "fat grant" so a group of "fatheads" can fool around for six months getting "fat" doing an idiotic study.

No Place for Soup-Slurpers

The question most often asked in this country today must be, "Smoking or non-smoking?" You hear it every time you step onto an airplane or a train, and some restaurants are beginning to separate customers who smoke from those who don't.

That's nothing. When you call for a taxi in New York, you can even request a non-smoking driver.

So determined are we to keep the two groups apart, I wouldn't be surprised if we eventually have smoking and non-smoking states.

The smokers, for instance, could all go live in industrial states where the air already is so foul they couldn't do any further damage to it.

Non-smokers could have what is left, like Montana, where the only pollution problem is an occasional moose with poor personal hygiene.

I happen to be a smoker, and I also happen to be an advocate of segregating smokers and non-smokers. One, I don't want to make anybody around me uncomfortable when I smoke, and two, who wants to be with an uppity group with clean lungs that probably also is into jogging and health foods and never has a light when you need one?

I also would like to take this whole idea a step further. If we are going to separate smokers from non-smokers in public places, why not make the same separation when it comes to other annoying habits?

Like throat-clearing in theaters and non-throat-clearing in theaters?

"Non-throat-clearing," I could answer, and be

removed forevermore from the jerk who apparently inhaled a pigeon and the feathers tickle his tonsils every time there is soft dialogue that needs to be followed closely.

I could go on. I think I will:

● Loud-talking in restaurants and non-loud-talking in restaurants.

Put me in the section where people came to eat, not to deliver the Gettysburg Address and other orations with mouths full of zucchini.

● Soup-slurping and non-soup-slurping.

Some people don't know how to eat soup. They fill their spoons too full and then, because the soup is hot, suck it into their mouths a small amount at a time.

That makes a slurping sound that is both annoying and crude. I would rather sit next to somebody who smells like a moose than somebody who slurps his soup.

● Nose-blowing and non-nose-blowing.

It should be against the law to blow your nose in public. It's not, so let's separate those who do from those who don't, especially when food is being served, soft music is being played, or there is to be a great deal of praying.

● Cosmetic-applying and non-cosmetic-applying.

I detest seeing a woman applying her paint and/or powder in the company of others. Seat those who would commit such a *faux pas* far from ordinary people who get sick at the smell of nail polish and at the sight of pooched lips awaiting a new coating of gloss, especially if it is that ghoulish lavender color disco queens and other vampires wear.

● Gum-chewing and non-gum-chewing.

Gum-chewers make loud, smacking noises, and they have a habit of throwing their gum on the floor when they are finished with it. Then I always come along and get it stuck on the bottom of my sneakers. That makes me want to kill gum-chewers.

For their own safety, put them off by themselves where, if they all want to sound like Secretariat enjoying an order of oats, nobody will hear them.

● Affection-displaying and non-affection-displaying.

You would be surprised how many couples nowadays wait until they are in a restaurant or a theater or on an airplane to play kissy-mouth and engage in all the squeezing and giggling that goes with it.

You don't think that can be disturbing? Look around you. Times, they are a-changin'—and the distraction is even greater when the two with the smoochies both have mustaches.

Running With Rosie

I admit I never had much interest in running until recently when I found out you can cheat at it. Now that I know you can cheat, I accept running as being a real sport.

Heretofore I thought it was just something bored housewives and guys who were in the drama club in high school did occasionally because they had never known the joy of sweating.

You can put in the fix in practically all our favorite athletic competitions. Baseball had its Black Sox scandal, basketball its point-shavings of the fifties, and somebody is always stealing a playbook in football, or doping a horse, or shooting an East German swimmer full of strange hormones.

But running? I never thought anybody cheated at running. I remember when some of my friends first started running.

"Who plays tennis or softball?" said one, an out-of-work actor. "Running is *pure*, man."

But then we come to the case of female runner Rosie Ruiz, the first woman to come across the finish line at the Boston Marathon, the Super Bowl of running.

Other runners, including the woman who finished second to her and spectators, claimed Rosie had not run the entire 26.2-mile course, but had slipped into the pack two miles from the finish line for a record time and a victory that is reportedly worth a lot of bucks in endorsements. Pure, man.

The stink caused a number of subsequent investigations and news conferences and a great deal of confusion. The problem, of course, is that the sport of running never has had to deal with a cheating scandal before and wasn't equipped to handle it.

What running needs to circumvent any such embarrassments in the future is a set of guidelines to follow in checking out finishing runners to make certain they completed the entire course.

The National Union for Running Development has offered a standby list of methods to be considered.

Following are some of the NURD suggestions:

● FOOT TEST: After twenty-six miles, a runner's feet should emit a certain odor. Each finishing runner will be asked to allow a foot judge to smell his or her feet. If the judge is rendered unconscious, there is a good chance the runner completed the entire course.

● JOGBRA TEST: No qualified female runner would attempt twenty-six miles without an official "jogbra." All the top women runners wear them. Any female finisher without such equipment should be detained for more questioning. Any male runner wearing a "jogbra" should be detained, period.

● SHOE TEST: Runners finishing in sandals, disco boots, moccasins, anything a cowboy might wear while walking the pasture, or barefooted should be considered suspicious. Any runner finishing in flip-flops should be placed in the same holding cage with the guys wearing "jogbras."

● BREATH TEST: Finishers who reek of

Gatorade or orange juice probably are legitimate. Finishers who reek of gin or vodka probably are just drunks who wandered out of the nearby bar to see what all the commotion was about.

● BURMA SHAVE TEST: "Burma Shave" signs will be posted every five miles along the course, and each finisher must be able to recite what appeared on each sign in order. For instance:

> *Here Sits Rosie,*
> *Brokenhearted.*
> *She Finished Fine,*
> *But She Never Started.*
> *Burma Shave.*

Lardbutts Need Love, Too

I went out to the baseball game the other night to watch the Braves lose, and I noticed local fans have formed the habit of booing Bob Horner.

For those of you who do not follow the sport, Bob Horner is this blond kid from out West someplace who is supposed to be some kind of whiz-bang player.

He's being paid three times what the president makes, but so far he hasn't produced returns proportionate to his pay.

For example, there was his performance the

night I caught his act. Four times he came to the plate with runners in scoring position in a tight game. Four times he looked like your Aunt Mildred trying to hit the ball.

There was also his defensive play. Your Aunt Mildred may not have Bob Horner's arm, but I'll bet she can cover more ground at third base.

I've heard all sorts of reasons for why Horner's play has been lacking. There was all that commotion over his contract, then Ted Turner wanted to demote him to Richmond at the first of the season, and he has had many injuries.

I always figured his biggest problem was he's a lardbutt. Lardbutts, because of the way they are built (bottom-heavy), have a difficult time in sports. Plus, despite the fact some of my best friends are lardbutts, they tend to be a little on the lazy side.

Roy Amos was a lardbutt, for instance. In the fifth grade, Roy Amos could hit the ball a long ways during recess games, but he would make somebody else run the bases for him. Also, Roy didn't like to bend over.

So that was my theory concerning Bob Horner: He's a lazy lardbutt who doesn't like to exert a lot of effort or bend over, just like Roy Amos.

But I was wrong, and when I am wrong I want to be the first to admit it. It was Horner's teammate, pitcher Al Hrabosky, who finally discovered the exact nature of Horner's problem.

Hrabosky has this radio show. When it was announced Horner would have to sit out a few days' games recently because of a "stomach disorder," Hrabosky said on his radio show it was not a stomach disorder at all, it was the dreaded "Heinekenitis."

I did some further checking and also learned that Horner picked up the "bug" one evening after a game in St. Louis.

How ashamed we all should be for booing him. A man in his condition cannot be expected to perform up to par.

And I should know. I, too, have had "Heinekenitis" and many other forms of it, such as "PBR Syndrome" and "Strohzema," both of which are just as painful, but don't cost as much to contract.

The symptoms normally begin when you awaken in the morning. They are headache, nausea, dizziness, nervousness, and you want to drink a lot of water, but you don't want to move around a lot or hear any loud noises.

Imagine a person being asked to catch a ground ball or run around a bunch of bases or listen to a screaming crowd in that condition.

When I have "Heinekenitis," it is a chore just to brush my teeth, but I do it anyway because another symptom is your mouth feels like the Chinese army spent the night there.

I think we all owe Bob Horner an apology. He is a sick man, doing the very best that he can, fighting a disease that has brought misery and suffering to millions.

Let us also remember the immortal words of Roy Amos, who said, "Lardbutts need love, too."

This is that apology, Bob. Hang in there, kid, and get well soon.

Forgiving the Bra-Padders

It would be easy to allow the case of Deborah Ann Fountain—the "little something extra girl" —to deflate and pass quietly into the void known as old news.

It never has been the nature of this column to turn its back when it senses that only the tip of a mammoth iceberg has been uncovered, however.

To refresh everyone's memory, Deborah Ann Fountain, Miss New York, went to Biloxi, Mississippi, to compete in the Miss U.S.A. beauty contest.

We all know how beauty contests work. A group of lovely young women strut around in nearly nothing for a couple of days and then a winner is picked, based on her talent and poise.

Miss Fountain decided she could improve her talent and poise by making it appear she had large breasts. So she stuck inch-thick padding into her swimsuit.

Competition can be very keen at a beauty contest. Miss Fountain's attempted trickery was discovered when a contest official, tipped by another contestant, went backstage and ripped down Miss Fountain's swimsuit and uncovered much more than just Miss Fountain.

How many other contest officials volunteered to go backstage and rip down Miss Fountain's swimsuit is not known.

Miss Fountain did what any red-blooded American beauty queen would do after such an experience. She filed suit. In her suit, she contended that four other contestants had silicone implants to boost their bust lines and that twenty other contestants had padded their bras too.

What concerns me is not Deborah Ann Fountain—she has padded her bra and now she must wear it—but just how common is this practice?

If twenty other contestants in the Miss U.S.A. pageant did, in fact, pad their bras, and four more had silicone implants, that means that half the field was cloaked in the dark veil of deceit.

What does this do for the credibility of other women who also are trying to cash in on their, well, talent and poise?

Dolly Parton, for instance. Say it ain't so, Dolly. Jane Russell, still doing bra commercials, and she remembers when Ronald Reagan was breaking in. Is that all you, Jane? And, heaven forbid, but was Janet Cooke wearing falsies when she wrote "Jimmy's World"?

There was a girl in my high school who learned a near-tragic lesson from attempting to be more than she was. During a vacation trip to the beach, she met a charming young man who asked her if she would like to take a swim in the surf.

She'd love to, she said, and met him on the

beach in a daring swimsuit. In order to impress the young man even more, she had padded the top of her suit to capacity.

As the two strolled into the surf, they suddenly stepped into much deeper water. The young man went all the way under and came to the surface gasping, only to find his companion not even neck-deep in water.

Before she could offer an explanation, the padding in her swimsuit sprang loose, and she sank quickly. Only the expert swimming abilities of her young man saved her from drowning.

I would suggest we now grant a National Day of Amnesty for all American women who have the courage to come forward and admit that they have in the past, or are presently, falsifying their pretenses.

This is a forgiving time in which we live. We will forgive Deborah Ann Fountain, of course, and we will forgive any other women who are willing to get it off their chests, so to speak.

We even forgave the girl in my high school, ol' what's-her-name with the floating swimsuit.

One Limeade for the Road

The Last Soda Fountain. Put it up there with *The Last Picture Show*, a marvelous motion picture, and with "The Last Cowboy Song," currently a raging country hit where Willie Nelson joins in on the last chorus.

But The Last Soda Fountain is neither a movie nor a song. It is reality.

The place was Springlake Pharmacy, and it was located near my home in Atlanta. There are memories.

Springlake Pharmacy is where I met Barney, my all-time favorite wino. Barney would sit outside Springlake on a slab of concrete and pour out his bottled dreams from a brown paper sack.

There was the day I saw two punks, they were maybe ten and eleven, throwing rocks at Barney. Barney wasn't bothering anybody. Barney was just drifting away for a time, and he was too weak and too drunk to dodge the rocks.

I chased the kids away. Barney thanked me by asking for a dollar.

Barney is dead now.

Springlake is where I bought toothpaste and shampoo and cough syrup and newspapers and once, when I forgot a rather special Valentine, one of those gaudy red boxes of chocolates she pretended to appreciate.

Springlake was where a person could belly-up to the counter of the honest-to-god, just-like-back-home-in-a-small-town soda fountain and ask and receive delights the likes of which are rare and precious indeed in the urban eighties.

Milkshakes. Not milkshakes out of some machine you have to eat with a spoon. That's not a milkshake. At Springlake, you got a milkshake constructed by a human hand scooping real ice cream into a cup with real milk, and you could *drink* the darn thing, as the Lord intended.

Limeade. Real limeade, made out of real lime juice, hand-squeezed from real limes. Thousands of limes were rendered juiceless over the years in Springlake. As far as I know, there is no other place in the continental United States that serves as good a limeade as did the soda fountain at Springlake.

I could go on. Cherry Cokes. Coca-Cola syrup, carbonated water and a shot of cherry juice. Good hot dogs. Ham sandwiches with thinly sliced tomatoes.

And nobody behind the counter wore stupid uniforms, and they didn't sell cookies in a funky little box, and the chicken noodle soup was called "chicken noodle soup." At some fastfood establishments today, chicken noodle soup would be called "Soup McNoodle."

My old pal, Estin, was numero uno behind the Springlake soda fountain counter. He spoke only when a grunt wouldn't do just as well.

And then there was the lady who worked with him. I never got her name. Somebody said she was Estin's niece. One day I ordered a ham sandwich and some potato chips from her. She delivered the ham sandwich. She forgot the potato chips, which were located on a rack behind the counter.

"You forgot my potato chips," I said.

"You got two legs," she replied. "Get your own potato chips."

It was that sort of friendly service that kept me coming back to Springlake, hallowed be its name.

Springlake, thirty-odd years at the same location, closed recently to the sound of a bulldozer's snort. A new shopping center went up next door, and the Springlake building was sold, and the Springlake owner decided to move his pharmacy and to pass the soda fountain along to the ages.

I walked inside for one last look.

"We're all just about in tears," said a lady helping dismantle the shelves. "It's a sad day."

The Last Soda Fountain. Let us mourn its leave, for nothing similar remains to take its place.

"Soup McNoodle." How utterly disgusting.

2

CORDIE MAE
AND THE GANG

It has been my pleasure to have known a lot of great, and near-great people in my time: Cordie Mae Poovey, Hog Phillpot, Kathy Sue Loudermilk, Mavis Boatright, all the Rainwaters—especially "Spot" and "Goat"—the late Curtis "Fruit Jar" Hainey, and my boyhood friend and idol, Weyman C. Wannamaker, Jr., a great American, who first showed me my way around in a 1957 Chevrolet....

CORDIE MAE
AND THE GANG

Hog Takes a Bride

What fun it has been keeping up with the big news in Britain: Prince Charles, who is thirty-two, is taking a bride, and she is cute, bubbly, nineteen-year-old Lady Diana Spencer, who giggles a lot.

The couple will marry in July, and some celebration it should be. I was trying to remember other big-deal marriages in the past, and I thought of Julie Nixon and David Eisenhower and Ari Onassis and Jackie Kennedy and Grace Kelly and Prince Rainier of Monaco, of course.

And then I remembered the one we had back home, when Harold "Hog" Phillpot married Cordie Mae Poovey, and everybody in town came. Pound for pound, it was the biggest wedding in the history of the county.

Hog tipped the Toledo at nearly 300. Nobody

ever knew exactly how much Cordie Mae weighed, but her daddy used to say, "If I could get $1.25 a pound for that child, I could pay off my truck."

Now that I think about it, Hog and Cordie Mae had a great deal in common with Prince Charles and Lady Diana.

Hog proposed in a garden, too, right in the middle of his daddy's collard patch, where Cordie Mae was picking a mess for her supper. Cordie Mae could eat a wheelbarrow load of collards and still want to fight you for yours. When Cordie Mae was hungry, she had the personality of a water buffalo with a gum boil.

Hog also was in his thirties when he married Cordie Mae, who was just nineteen, like Lady Diana. Cordie Mae wasn't one to giggle very much, however. When she laughed she made a sound like a dump truck being cranked on a cold morning.

I don't know the exact plans of Prince Charles and Lady Diana's wedding, but if it is anything like Hog and Cordie Mae's, it will be a dandy. I managed to locate a yellowed clipping from the local newspaper that described the event:

"Mr. and Mrs. Lark Poovey take pride in announcing the marriage of their daughter, Cordie Mae, to Mr. Harold "Hog" Phillpot, son of Mr. and Mrs. Grover Phillpot, at the Mt. Giliad Free Will Baptist Church Saturday, April 11, 1959, at three o'clock in the afternoon.

"The groom is a graduate of the Nuway Re-cap School and currently is employed by Elroy's

Gulf and Tire as Elroy's night manager. The bride, former state high school girls' wrestling champion (heavyweight division), is the popular bouncer at the Gateway Recreation Hall and Beer Joint.

"The wedding service was delivered by the Rev. Vernon 'Jericho' Walls, and the bride was given away by her father, a prominent sheetrocker and dog breeder. Miss Teeter Combs played several selections on the organ, including the traditional 'Wedding March' and her speciality, 'On Wisconsin.'

"The bride's outfit was designed by Arnold's Tent and Awning Co. The happy couple exited the church under crossed lug wrenches, held by employees from Elroy's Gulf and Tire.

"The reception was held in the basement of the church, where the Rev. Walls' wife, Sharinda, served Hawaiian Punch to one and all. Following a wedding trip to the nearest Burger Chef, the couple will reside in the Lonesome Pines Trailer Park, Row Five, Trailer M, a handsome double-wide."

It's hard to believe it's been more than twenty years since Hog and Cordie Mae got married. They're still together, incidentally, but they had to move from Lonesome Pines into a house. Cordie Mae gained so much more weight that she was wider than the trailer.

Mean Mo-Sheen

The Chrysler Corporation has made another big decision. It no longer will produce those big ugly cars nobody will buy—heaps like the Chrysler Newport, the Dodge St. Regis, or the Plymouth Grand Fury, whatever that is.

From now on, Chrysler will produce only intermediate-sized ugly cars nobody will buy. Won't somebody do Chrysler a big favor and pull its plug for good?

I've known for a long time why Chrysler can't sell cars. It has nothing to do with size. It is because Chrysler is trying to sell cars to a generation it never bothered to impress when we were in high school.

Nobody in my school would have been caught dead driving a Chrysler. The principal always drove a Chrysler, or something like it—a DeSoto, for instance, which was worse than one of those fat, black Buicks with the holes in the sides.

The shop teacher, meanwhile, usually was the one with the pale blue Plymouth without chrome or a radio, and the band director drove a brown Dodge.

How can all that possibly affect Chrysler today? Don't you see? It is in high school that a person, especially a boyperson, first gets hooked on cars. It is during that period he forms certain attitudes and makes certain value judgments concerning automobiles that he will carry into manhood.

In the late fifties and early sixties, you couldn't have gotten a date with Cordie Mae Poovey, the ugliest girl in school, driving a Chrysler.

Now we all are grown, but the anti-Chrysler feelings linger, so we're all out buying those little Japanese imports, which we really don't want—but at least there is no chance of being mistaken for a shop teacher in one.

I have a couple of suggestions for Chrysler that could save the farm.

One, forget all the plans for the intermediate-sized cars, or any-sized cars that look like anything you have built in the past two decades. Face it. Those dogs won't hunt.

Two, beg, borrow, or steal the designs to the greatest car ever made. Produce something that at least closely resembles it, and in six months, I promise you will have won over the entire generation of customers you blew twenty years ago.

I am speaking of the 1957 Chevrolet.

There never has been such another car as the '57 Chevy. Its lines were classic, and its back seat was roomy. Its grillwork and fins said, "Here is power, here is speed." And its back seat was roomy.

It was THE car of my youth. A guy driving a 1957 Chevrolet could get a date with ANY girl in school, up to, and including, Kathy Sue Loudermilk, the Collard Festival queen.

I never owned a '57 Chevy, but my boyhood friend and idol, Weyman C. Wannamaker, Jr., a great American, did. A convertible. A red one. Hottamighty, what a car!

He had "Sassy Chassis" written on the hood, and he had flames painted on each door. Weyman called his car his "mean mo-sheen," and occasionally he even would allow me to drive this piece of automotive genius, like when he was busy discussing an upcoming algebra exam in the roomy back seat with Kathy Sue Loudermilk.

I can hear Weyman now, giving me instructions on how to drive his car. "Eyes forward, stupid," he used to say.

So maybe it's a long shot, Chrysler, but nothing else has worked. Give Americans a mosheen like the '57 Chevy and maybe they will remember there are some things in a car more important than gas mileage. And maybe they will tell the Japanese to go eat some fish heads.

Besides, their stupid little cars with those cramped back seats have been taking the fun out of American automobiling long enough.

Making Sense of the Census

What I like most about the taking of the census is that it's fair. Once every ten years everybody counts, and everybody counts the same:

One.

Even Bo Derek. Imagine, Bo Derek a "one." Somehow, I can't imagine that.

Something else I like about the census: It's thorough. Most Americans probably mailed in their census reports April 1, but canvassers soon will be going into places like pool halls, dives, and fleabag hotels in big cities to count heads.

That is important because, otherwise, a pool shark or a wino could be missed. The last time there was a census, for instance, my boyhood friend and idol, Weyman C. Wannamaker, Jr., a great American and part-time pool shark and wino, wasn't counted. He was taking a nap (passed out) underneath a load of turnips in the back of his pickup truck when the census-taker came around.

I can't wait for the results of the census to be released. I realize a great deal of the information we gave the government is supposed to be kept confidential, but this census thing is costing the taxpayers a bundle, so why shouldn't we be privy to some of the juicier material?

I just happen to have with me a list of questions I would like answered by the census:

● The 1980 census had the audacity to ask people if they have indoor plumbing. Did any of my neighbors mark "no"? (I have always suspected the Bloomingraths. They spend an awful lot of time going back and forth to Mr.

Bloomingrath's "tool shed," and they never have any beer parties.)

● Does anybody really live in North Dakota?

● What is the population of my hometown, Moreland, Georgia? The last time there was a census taken, there were 300-plus, but that was before the Rainwater family moved out. (There were so many Rainwaters, they ran out of names for the last four children and had to name them after dogs in the neighborhood. "Spot" Rainwater was one of my closest friends.)

● How many teen-agers are there in America, and when will they all grow up so rock music will finally die out?

● Ten million people live in New York City, where the air is foul, the streets are dirty and the weather is terrible. Hardly anybody lives in Yellville, Arkansas, where the mountain air is refreshing, there are many streams and rivers for fishing and boating and swimming naked, and you don't' have to lock your doors at night. Why?

● Who is the oldest person in America, and has he or she ever jogged?

● Under "sex," how many people put down "undecided," and are any of them in my tennis club?

● How many people in America are named "Engelbert Humperdink"?

● Did the name "D.B. Cooper" show up anywhere?

● When is my wife's birthday?

● And, finally, just exactly how many people do live in this country, and with the government doing the counting, how can I be certain that figure is correct?

I can't. If the government knew beans about simple arithmetic, it wouldn't just now be balancing its own checkbook for the first time since it was taking the 1960 census.

Incidentally, they missed Weyman C. Wannamaker, Jr., in 1960, too. He hid in the family "tool shed," which used to be none of the government's damn business.

Pucker Princess of '62

A jeweler friend of mine mentioned recently you can get as much as $150 by digging out your old high school class ring and selling it at what still remains a good price for gold.

I really hate to use this forum for something so personal, but I haven't been able to find my old high school class ring, and I just remembered what happened to it.

What happened to it was Mavis Boatright, a girl in my school, the night at the drive-in movie when I asked her to go steady. Going steady with Mavis Boatright, which nearly everybody did at one time or the other, meant French kissing her on the mouth if you came across with something of value she could wear to impress her girlfriends.

"How about my letter jacket?" was my first offer, during the intermission between *Gidget Goes Hawaiian* and some Doris Day thing I wanted to French kiss on the mouth through with Mavis Boatright.

"What sport?" she asked.

"Debate," I answered, proudly.

"Pass," said Mavis, who was not exceedingly intellectual, but her parents allowed her to stay out until midnight, thus giving her great bargaining powers.

Plus, the girl could kiss. A Mavis Boatright lip-lock was something to behold.

My next offer was my foam-rubber dice that hung from the rearview mirror of my car, but Marvin Waterman had made the same offer the night before, and Mavis had told him to go French kiss a bird dog, which is exactly what she told me. Mavis had some kind of quick wit about her.

"How about the ring?" she finally asked.

I was afraid she would ask that. Getting a boy's class ring meant it was something really serious, something that might last as long as a month. I didn't want to spend an eternity with Mavis Boatright, I just wanted to press my lips tenderly against hers and feel the tinge of excitement run down my spine as she bent my head against the movie speaker.

"I can't give you my class ring," I said.

"So we'll sit here and watch Doris Day go on a crying jag for two hours," Mavis responded.

I gave her my class ring, and my lips were numb for a week. It wasn't long after that, however, she ran off with Marvin Waterman and got married, and she never bothered to return my ring.

Now, I want my ring back. I've tried everything to locate her, including calling around in my hometown, but nobody has any idea whatever happened to Mavis and Marvin.

This is simply a shot in the dark, a last-ditch effort. Maybe you will read this, Mavis, and return my ring.

These are difficult times, and, quite frankly, I could use the cash it would bring. I'm planning a small cookout for a few friends, and the 150 big ones would just about cover the buns and pickle relish.

There also is a matter of principle here, Mavis, and you know what I'm talking about. After That Night, you told every girl in school that kissing me was like drinking warm buttermilk.

Do you realize how long it was before I got kissed again after that? Do you realize how many Doris Day movies I had to sit through after that? Do you know I got so sick of Doris Day that every time she started one of her crying jags I wanted Rock Hudson to bash her one?

That's exactly what I would like to do to you, Mavis. Bam! Right in your kisser, legend that it was. Bitter, Mavis, is the man scorned and $150 in the hole for one night of passion with the pucker princess of 1962, wherever you are.

"When It's Refill Time in Heaven"

I stopped for lunch in one of those meat-and-three vegetables places the other day and, much to my surprise, the waitress brought my iced tea in a quart fruit jar.

You don't see that sort of thing any more, but fruit jars have a significant history, and I even get a little sentimental when I think about them. More about that later.

First, for those who are not familiar with the fruit jar, it is a wide-mouthed, glass container normally associated with the process of canning, as in the canning of vegetables and fruits.

These containers also may be called "Mason" jars for the name of the company that produces state-of-the-art fruit jars. But people who say "Mason jar" instead of "fruit jar" probably are a little snooty and sleep in pajamas.

In the past, in certain parts of rural America, it was quite common for people who couldn't afford regular glassware—and slept in their underwear—to use these fruit jars as part of their table settings

You take a family in my hometown, the Rainwaters. The Rainwaters were too poor to afford glasses, so Mrs. Rainwater always served beverages in fruit jars.

Claude "Goat" Rainwater was one of my best friends, despite the fact that he rarely bathed. Mrs. Rainwater would serve Goat his food and his fruit jar on the back porch with the dog.

There are certain advantages to drinking from a fruit jar.

The wide mouth allows easy intake of the liquid inside the jar, whether it be iced tea, buttermilk, lemonade, or something more potent.

It is so easy to drink from a fruit jar, as a matter of fact, that it is virtually impossible to keep whatever you are drinking from pouring over your chin, down your neck, and onto the front of your shirt.

There was a man who lived in the woods near my hometown who sold a certain beverage that was so potent you wanted to be careful not to get any on your shirt because it would ruin your shirt. It would eat through sandpaper and cut out engine knock, too.

As I finished my lunch and poured down the last of my iced tea from my fruit jar, my sentimentality got the best of me as I thought of one of my favorite people from my youth.

I am speaking of the late, great Curtis "Fruit Jar" Hainey. Fruit Jar got that name because he was never without one stuck in his coat or in his back pocket.

It usually was filled with the clear liquid—and

an occasional bug or leaf the strainer missed—
that he purchased from the aforementioned
man in the woods.

I can see ol' Fruit Jar now, ambling along.

"Where you headed, Fruit Jar?" we would
ask.

"Refill time," he would answer, smiling and
holding up his empty jar as he headed for the
woods.

Fruit Jar spent so much time drinking there
was a notch on his nose from where the top of
his jar pressed against it.

"That stuff's gonna kill him someday," the
women from the church used to say.

Sure enough, it did. He went one jar over the
line one cold night. The blind girl wrote a song
for him and sang it at the funeral after the
preacher got through. She called it "Lord, Remember Fruit Jar When It's Refill Time in
Heaven."

Goat Rainwater even took a bath for the ser-
vices. A man like Curtis "Fruit Jar" Hainey
doesn't die every day.

The Birth of the Jeans Craze

There is an awful lot of conversation these days
concerning the case of fifteen-year-old actress-
model Brooke Shields and her pair of tight-
fitting Calvin Klein jeans.

Miss Shields made a commercial in her tight-fitting Calvin Kleins and also made a few, ahem, suggestive remarks.

The public was outraged. The commercials were yanked off television.

This accomplished two things:

● It made Miss Shields, whose talent is not exactly legendary, into a big star. Her previous accomplishments included playing the role of twelve-year-old hooker and getting stranded on an island with nothing but her ragged loincloth and somebody who was a boy but wasn't her brother. Brooke Shields is fifteen going on thirty-five.

● It sold the diddly out of Calvin Klein jeans.

Frankly, I don't know what the fuss is all about. For years, blossoming young women have been fitting themselves into blue jeans two sizes too small for them. Women just naturally do something to a pair of jeans that a hairy-legged boy can't.

You take Kathy Sue Loudermilk, for instance. It was Kathy Sue Loudermilk who started the blue-jean craze that is now sweeping the world.

She actually wore the first pair of designer jeans ever made to the annual Fourth of July Barbecue and Street Dance in my hometown on July 5, 1954. (July 4 got rained out that year.)

Her jeans were designed by her mother, the former Edna Pearl Simpkins, who fashioned them from a flour sack.

Unfortunately—or fortunately—Edna Pearl

didn't quite have enough sack to fit Kathy Sue, and she came up a couple of sizes too small.

When Kathy Sue arrived at the dance, the band stopped playing, people stopped dancing, the Baptist preacher broke into a prodigious sweat, and Goot Niles swallowed a brand-new plug of Brown Mule chewing tobacco.

Of course, there was some outrage expressed concerning Kathy Sue's outfit back then, too. The ladies of the church passed around a petition to ban Kathy Sue's britches from future town gatherings and gave it to the Baptist preacher, who had to drink two quarts of lemonade to cool down every time Kathy Sue's name was mentioned.

"Let's be sensible, ladies," the preacher said. "She's only a child."

"My grandmother's hat," said Goot Niles' wife, Ruby Jean, who also chewed Brown Mule.

Finally the preacher said he would speak to Kathy Sue's mother, Edna Pearl, but by that time she was already working on sack jeans for almost every young woman in town.

Even Cordie Mae Poovey got a pair. Cordie Mae was a big girl who sort of reminded you of a semi hauling hogs. It took five flour sacks and seven yards of elastic for Edna Pearl to make Cordie Mae's jeans.

"The Blob! It lives!" said my boyhood friend and idol, Weyman C. Wannamaker, Jr., a great American, the first time he saw Cordie Mae in her new outfit. She kneed him in the belly and sat on him until it was nearly dark.

When people got too sophisticated to buy their flour in large cloth sacks, Edna Pearl had to get out of the jeans business.

Too bad. Brooke Shields in a pair of Calvin Kleins is kid stuff. Kathy Sue Loudermilk in a pair of Edna Pearls would make a good man leave home, or Cordie Mae Poovey wasn't two sizes bigger than a train wreck.

3

BOY COLUMNIST

There are many lessons to be learned from the following chapter, such as how to inspect the cap of a wine bottle before you screw it off, where to get a good tattoo, what to do with your polyester leisure suits, how to tell whether or not something that goes bump in the night is about to get you, and where grits come from. This is a very intellectual chapter ....

Drinkin' Wine, Spodee-Odee

I have been checking around, and I have unearthed an incredible discovery: Very few newspapers have a wine columnist.

How absurd. Do newspapers not realize more and more Americans are drinking wine these days? Do they not realize there has been a tremendous increase in the number of wine commercials on television? And think how many fat, out-of-work actors that has helped.

Wine. What an intriguing subject. There have been odes written on it, and songs written about it, as the classic Jerry Lee Lewis rendition of:

> *Drinkin' wine, spodee-odee,*
> *Drinkin' wine.*
> *Drinkin' wine, spodee-odee,*
> *Drinkin' wine.*

> *Drinkin' wine, spodee-odee,*
> *Drinkin' wine.*
> *Pass 'at bottle to me.*

Historically, wine-drinking songs rely more on a catchy tune than lyrical quality.

By now you are probably saying to yourself, "Hey, this guy really knows his wine." But, of course.

I go way back with wine, back to when I was thirteen and I went off with my boyhood friend and idol, Weyman C. Wannamaker, Jr., a great American, who had swiped a bottle of something called Eleven Cellars, a rather indelicate port, from the storeroom of the local beer joint.

"Shall you taste, or shall I?" asked Weyman as he unscrewed the cap.

"Be my guest," I said.

"It's a good wine, but not a great wine," said Weyman after the first chug. "The bouquet leaves something to be desired, but its mood is rich."

Indeed. I required medical attention before the day was out. I told my mother I had been eating persimmons.

My knowledge and appreciation of wine was enhanced by a close association with one of the nation's leading wine experts, Ralph (High-Lift) Turnipseed.

When I was a kid, the county in which I lived was dry. That is, you had to buy your booze from a bootlegger in order to keep the church people happy.

One week the local bootlegger went on vacation, and Ralph was left without his normal supply of wine. So he drank Vitalis instead. After that, when he walked, he always picked up one of his legs much higher than the other. Thus, "High-Lift."

High-Lift preferred what he called "walking-around wine," a half-pint of just about anything that would flow downhill. Half-pint bottles would fit in his back pocket, and he therefore would not be bothered by having to carry around a large paper sack.

When he was sixty-five, the doctors told High-Lift he wouldn't live another six months if he didn't slow down on his drinking. So he started drinking a lot faster after that and, sure enough, he was nearly eighty when he died. In a motorcycle accident.

Anyway, what this country needs is a good wine columnist and, once again, I must step in to fill the void. Here are a few tips to remember about wine from my very first wine column:

● Always check to see if the seal of the cap is intact before you allow the waiter to unscrew the cap off the bottle. If the seal has been broken, chances are the help has been nipping from the bottle back in the kitchen and may have refilled the portion they drank with water or 7-Up.

● Remember, it's white wine for fish or poultry, red wine for meat. For sardines and soda crackers in the alley, a nice, slightly pink MD 20-20 (any month) is certainly acceptable.

● Never order Wild Russian Vanya unless there is a CPR expert in the restaurant.

● If you're ever in Terre Haute, call EV-7-4433 and ask for Gladys. What's that got to do with wine? Take her a bottle of Gallo Thunderbird and you'll see.

Next time I will discuss what kind of paper cups are best when serving Cold Duck.

The Secrets of My Past

My admiration for Dan Rather, heir to CBS anchorman Walter Cronkite, went up a notch when I read he had admitted in an interview with *The Ladies Home Journal* he has used heroin.

"Not socially," says Rather, but "so I could write a story about it" when he worked in Houston.

Rather also said the experience was "a special kind of hell."

It is only right that a newsman of Rather's stature, who is entrusted with the faith and admiration of millions who watch him dole out the evening news, makes public any previously hidden incidents in his past that could be unveiled later and possibly cause him to lose credibility and respect.

We ask our politicians to open their backgrounds and checkbooks to public scrutiny, so why shouldn't we expect the same from our newspersons?

I'm glad I asked that question, because I am here today to make my life an open book, just like Dan Rather.

As a reader, you have every right to know whether I am a sane, normal person or whether I am some kind of dope-headed sicko who probably has been arrested a couple of times and doesn't like football.

We will do this in the form of an interview. First question, please:

Q. Have you ever "experimented" with drugs?

A. Yes. As part of a general science project in the seventh grade, I fed my neighbor's cat six bottles of aspirin to see what effect the six bottles of aspirin would have on a cat.

Q. And your findings?

A. After eating six bottles of aspirin, a cat will lie very still.

Q. You are evading the real question here. Have you, yourself, ever indulged in an illegal drug, such as marijuana?

A. I cannot tell a lie. Once at a party in Chicago I was with some weird people, and the host, who wore a lot of neck chains and didn't button the front of his shirt, passed around a marijuana cigarette to all his guests.

When it came my turn, the cigarette was very short. I attempted to smoke it, but I sucked the fire into my mouth, instead.

Marijuana causes large blisters on your tongue, so I don't smoke it any more.

Q. Have you ever been arrested?

A. No, but once I received a substantial penalty for early withdrawal from my passbook savings account. The bank teller hit me in the mouth.

Q. Have you ever undergone treatment for a psychiatric disorder?

A. That was in the third grade when the county health teacher was called in to question me concerning why I wouldn't go out of the building during recess to play with the rest of the children.

Q. And what did the health teacher find was your problem?

A. I was scared stiff of Cordie Mae Poovey, the meanest girl in school, who used to pound on my head during recess because she didn't like my looks.

Q. Do you ever drink to excess?

A. Only on weeknights. On weekends, I get blitzed.

Q. Are there any abnormal sexual tendencies in your background?

A. No, but I had a cousin who was a thespian.

Q. Is there anything more you would like to add to this investigation?

A. Just one more thing. When I wrote this column I was high on a plate of Uncle Sam's Red-Hot Texas Chili.

What's Preppy and What Ain't

If you haven't picked up your copy of *The Official Preppy Handbook*, you absolutely must do so. Otherwise you might commit some horrid *faux pas* such as entering the wrong school, thereby being cursed for life as a member of the Great Unwashed.

For those who still are not certain exactly what a preppy is, he or she is a person who was to the manor born, so to speak, who is aware of all the social graces—and disgraces—and who always wears just the right clothing, goes to just the right vacation spots, and, of course, belongs to just the right clubs.

A snob, in other words.

It is important to know who and what is preppy today, since the ruling class has taken over the country again.

The Official Preppy Handbook, currently a runaway best seller, goes for the modest price of $3.95. But even at that, a lot of people probably will never get around to purchasing a copy of *TOPH*, and that concerns me greatly.

Who will lead the masses out of their ignorance? Who will tell the working class to turn up the collars on their pink Izods, to always keep a reserve pair of deck shoes and to name their children Muffy, Corkie, and Topsy (girls) and Chip, Kip, and Trip (boys)?

Many citizens, especially those whose club affiliations are with organizations bearing the names of large, hairy animals found in Canada, don't have the slightest idea that they should always wear gray flannels when having lunch at the Palm Court with Grandmother.

I am here to help these people. "Grizzard's Guide to What's Preppy and What Ain't" is available right here in this very column for free. So save your $3.95 and go buy a couple of six-packs of *brewskis,* an official preppy term for beer. Drinking beer is certainly preppy, as long as you don't do it between bouts at the wrestling matches.

CLOTHING: Throw away anything that resembles polyester, even relatives with stretch marks. A preppy wouldn't wear polyester to a ditch dig. Men, khaki is always safe, and women should stick to shirtdresses, wrap skirts and Calvin Klein jeans.

Women should never wear tank tops, especially if they have tattoos that would be exposed.

SCHOOLING: If you currently are enrolled in the Columbia School of Broadcasting, Harold's College of Transmission Repair, any public school, any barber school, or the University of Arkansas, you probably should commit suicide, or at least stay home nights.

CLUBS: When you hear the term "Junior

League," do you think of (a) a spiffy women's service organization or (b) what the Kansas City Royals play in? If you answered "b," the Kiwanis wouldn't have you.

HOBBIES: The favorite hobbies of preppies are things like bird watching and collecting Chinese porcelain and Franklin Mint coins. Sorry, no preppy ever square-danced.

MONEY: You need a lot of this to be a preppy. Take the following test to see if you qualify:

1. Is L.L. Bean (a) the senior senator from Idaho now that Frank Church is gone, (b) a vegetable, (c) a promising middleweight contender, or (d) a famous place in Maine where preppies like to shop?

2. Is Dom Perignon (a) a baseball player from someplace like Cuba, (b) a disease of the esophagus, (c) the CBS correspondent from Ankara, or (d) a very expensive champagne?

3. Is Perrier (a) Ronald Reagan, Jr.'s, best pal at dancing school, (b) the capital of South Dakota, (c) a nasal decongestant, or (d) bottled water preppies drink when they have a hangover?

If you answered anything but "d" on any question, go wait in the truck, Ripple-breath.

Dr. Feelbad

I was browsing through the papers when I ran across an interesting, but alarming, statistic: twenty percent of the medical costs in the country are being paid out by hypochondriacs—people who are convinced they are sick, but nobody will listen to them, especially doctors.

I have been a practicing hypochondriac for years, and I can't begin to tell you of the suffering. I have had symptoms of every known disease, but never have I been able to find a doctor who agrees with my diagnosis.

Like the time I had toe cancer. Toe cancer is when your little toe becomes swollen and sort of bent out of shape and hurts when you walk.

I went to my doctor, convinced my toe would have to be removed that afternoon, but hoping the leg, at least, could be saved.

My doctor took one look at my toe and said my shoes were too tight. So I changed to a half-size larger shoe, and my toe got better, proving loose shoes to be a definite cure for toe cancer.

This twenty percent thing bothers me because that is a bundle of money for hypochondriacs to be paying out to doctors to be told nothing is wrong with, us. Hypochondriacs don't go to doctors to be told nothing is wrong; they go to be assured something most certainly is.

I think I have a solution to the problem. Rather than a doctor, what hypochondriacs need is another hypochondriac—like me, for instance—to tell them they are just as sick as they think they are, which would make them very happy.

And think of the money they would save in doctor bills.

Maybe I could write the first newspaper advice column for hypochondriacs. They send in their symptoms, and I use my many years' experience diagnosing my own health problems to diagnose theirs.

Let's give it a practice run. I'll be "Dr. Feelbad, the hypochondriac's best friend," and the column would work something like this:

Dear Dr. Feelbad: After playing tennis, I get a terrible pain in my elbow. My doctor says all I have is common "tennis elbow." But I think it is something much worse. Which of us is correct?

—D.A., Pittsburgh, Pa.

Dear D.A.: You are. What does your doctor know about tennis? You don't have tennis "elbow." You have tennis "arm," and it probably will have to be amputated eventually, and you won't be able to play tennis. You will become a recluse and have to sit around staring out the window all the time. Have a nice day.

Dear Dr. Feelbad: I have a terrible headache. My wife says it is because I got smashed last night, but I know better. I know it probably is a brain tumor and I won't live until

morning. How do I break the news to my wife?
—**Checking Out, Mobile, Ala.**

Dear Checking Out: Your diagnosis is absolutely correct. But wait until you and your wife are in bed and then break the bad news to her gently. But don't keep her up too late. Remember, she has to get up in the morning. You don't.

Dear Dr. Feelbad: I know the seven danger signals of cancer, and I worry about them all the time. But are there any others I could be worrying about, too? I'm getting bored with the first seven.

—**Betty, Laredo, Texas**

Dear Betty: You bet your boots there are. Here are some of my other favorite danger signals to worry about: Drowsiness toward midnight, increase in bellybutton lint, and sudden loss of memory after a half-dozen tequila shooters.

Dear Dr. Feelbad: Last evening I experienced chest pains and difficulty breathing. Incidentally, my girlfriend, Bearnice, who weighs 300 pounds, was sitting on me at the time. Could I have heart trouble?
—**Slim, Terre Haute, Ind.**

Dear Slim: Probably not. Bearnice's last boyfriend wrote in about the same thing, but all his problem turned out to be was four broken ribs, bruised kidneys, and a squashed liver. Sorry, better luck next time.

Mr. Cool

A couple of dashing young fellows named Gregory Smith White and Steve Woodward Naifeh have written a book on what men should do to be cool.

The book is titled *Moving Up in Style*, and it teaches men how to dress, what to order in a fancy restaurant, and why scratching your privates in public isn't such a good idea.

The only problem with the book is it is too expensive. It costs $10.95. For $10.95, you could buy a case of beer or take a date to the wrestling match.

Who's got $10.95 to blow on some dumb book that gets all involved in what wines are from where and which ones you should drink with what? Just remember not to order a bottle with a screw-off top, and you can't go wrong.

What I am getting around to is this: I know a great deal about being cool myself, having been to three state fairs and to Daytona Beach when I was in high school.

I also know why this distasteful ethnic joke is supposed to be funny:

What are they drinking these days in Poland? Perrier and water.

So there is absolutely no reason to go out and blow $10.95 on Gregory Whozits and Steve Whatshisface's book when, for the price of this newspaper, you can read my occasional "Mr. Cool" column where male readers write in and ask questions concerning style and good taste.

Are you a male? Do you have a question concerning style and good taste? If so, write "Mr. Cool," in care of me, and if you're lucky, I'll pick your question to answer, and all your friends will get to see your name in print.

Incidentally, a couple of bucks in the envelope and Mr. Cool will personally see to it that you get lucky, which still saves you nearly nine dollars.

Here is the Mr. Cool column for today, just to give you an idea of how the deal works:

Dear Mr. Cool: I am thirty-two and have been dating my current girlfriend, who is twenty-five, for six months. So far, we have not kissed because I am afraid of where it could lead. Has it been long enough that I should go ahead and give in? Mom says "no." —**Skippy Winthrop III, Spartanburg, S.C.**

Dear Skippy: If you're as dippy as you sounded in your letter, I doubt if kissing could lead anywhere but to total revulsion for your girlfriend, who obviously is after you for your bucks.

So tell your Mom to take a hike. Just remember, while you're kissing, it's not cool to peep to see if she has her eyes closed.

Dear Mr. Cool: Me and my woman, Betty Louann Sue, went out drinking the other night. I ordered us two cans of beer, and the waitress brought us two glasses. I know one of the glasses was for Betty Louann Sue to drink her PBR out of, but what was the other one for?—**Ronnie Ray Tucker, Vidalia, Ga.**

Dear Ronnie Ray: The answer to that question would only confuse you. Go put another quarter in the juke box and punch E-4, "We Used to Kiss on the Lips, But It's All Over Now."

Dear Mr. Cool: Is it ever permissible to wear white socks?—**Harley Fingers, Birmingham, Ala.**

Dear Harley: Certainly. While hanging out at the Moose Lodge or attending your bowling team's annual banquet, for instance. Also, white socks may be worn with anything made of polyester, or anybody named Betty Louann Sue.

Dear Mr. Cool: What is the proper wine to serve with Boston Scrod?—**Telly Cervantes, Malibu, Calif.**

Dear Telly: Anybody who would eat something called "scrod" wouldn't know the difference. Start with Ripple and work your way down.

Dear Mr. Cool: I want to get a tattoo. All my friends—Butch, Leroy, and Killer—have them. Butch and Leroy have theirs on their forearms. Killer has his on his chest. Where is the best place to get a tattoo?—**Bevo Scrump, Palatka, Fla.**

Dear Bevo: Pete's Transmission Shop and Tattoo Parlor, West Memphis, Ark.

Wrong Shade of Red

Since I have been writing a column, I have been called a lot of names.

"Redneck" is a favorite among many of my loyal readers.

"You redneck, why don't you ride off into the sunset in your pickup?" they write when they particularly enjoy one of my columns.

"Buzzard" is another favorite, because it sort of sounds like my name. Actually, "buzzard" and "Griz-ZARD," which is the way my father taught me to pronounce my name, don't sound alike at all, but they sort of look alike, which is enough for me to get ten or twenty letters a week that begin:

"Dear Buzzard, I will never read your column again."

What is interesting about that is two weeks later, I receive another batch of hate mail from the same creeps, uh, fans.

Anyway, this is all leading up to something, I think, and that is to inform you that for the first time in my career, I have been called a "communist."

Actually, I have been called even more than that. I have been called a "liberal, socialistic communist," which is really calling somebody something, like when you say a person is a "dumb, hillbilly redneck" or a "lizard, gizzard buzzard."

Robert E. Crout of Greenville, South Carolina, an important textile town located somewhere near Interstate 85, is the one who called me that name.

He wrote a letter to my editor that said, "It is my firm opinion that the majority of readers with common sense are tired of the liberal, socialistic, communist view of Lewis Grizzard."

My editor, who is a close friend of mine, couldn't wait to publish that letter.

What had Mr. Crout so upset, apparently, was the fact that I recently published a copy of the official senility test they are going to give Ronald Reagan, who is nearly as old as baseball, when he starts forgetting things like where he sent Alexander Haig and why.

"It is about time," continued Mr. Crout's letter, "all of us begin to remember a few of the 'Communist Rules for Revolution'....

"'Get control of all means of publicity and thereby divide the people into hostile groups by constantly harping on controversial matters of no importance and destroy people's faith in their natural leaders by holding (them) up to contempt, ridicule and obloquy.'"

My mother read that letter. So did my wife, and my minister, and maybe even both of my ex-mothers-in-law, who probably made copies and passed them around.

I demand equal time:

Mr. Crout, I am a lot of things. A Methodist, for instance. But I am not now, nor have I ever been, a commie. I have never read the "Communist Rules for Revolution," as you quite obviously have. I don't even know who wrote them.

Furthermore, how could I be a good commie if I don't even know what "obloquy" is? It probably is some swill of a soup they serve to poor suckers who get sent to Siberia.

Mr. Crout, I was a Boy Scout and a Little Leaguer. The only political parties in which I involve myself are election-night bashes with free food and booze. I own two "America: Love It or Leave It" bumper stickers, and I know all the words to Merle Haggard's patriotic ditty, "Walkin' on the Fightin' Side of Me."

I love the memory of John Wayne, the Dodgers, hot dogs with mustard, apple pie a la mode (even when you can't get any ice cream to put on it), my mother, college football, fuzzy puppies, cold beer, and courthouse squares. Walter Cronkite gives me goose pimples.

I don't drink vodka, and I once observed that Russian women give the plain-toed work boots they wear a bad name.

Me, a rotten, pinko commie? That's a hoot. Whoever heard of a commie in a pickup? They ride around in those foreign-made vans with slogans printed all over the side. Everybody knows that.

So go take a brain scan to see if anything shows up, Mr. Kraut, or Mr. Croop, or whatever your name was. Better yet, go stick your head in a bucket of obloquy.

Cooter Brown Award

The time has come to announce the winner of the First Annual Drunk-As-Cooter Brown Award. The award is named for the immortal Cooter Brown, who could get drunker than anybody.

Once Cooter got so drunk he wandered into the middle of a church service and began babbling incoherently.

"Praise the Lord!" somebody screamed out. "That man is speaking in tongues!"

"No, he's not," said somebody else. "It's just Cooter Brown trying to sing, 'There Stands the Glass.'"

"There Stands the Glass," I might explain, is a Webb Pierce classic, a favorite of many a drinking man.

This award, conceived by me, neither encourages nor condones drinking, but I do feel if someone distinguishes himself in that area, he should not go unrecognized.

The winner of the First Annual Drunk-As-Cooter Brown Award goes to a fellow I know, Rigsby, who got so drunk on a recent business trip that he checked into his hotel twice.

"Nobody gets that drunk," I said.

"Yes, they do," said Rigsby, "I got off the airplane, went straight to my hotel and checked in. But I didn't go to my room. I met some business associates in the bar, and we proceeded to drink for several hours.

"We got pretty much oiled and decided to go somewhere for dinner. I drove my rental car. I parked it in front of this brick wall.

"When we came out of the restaurant, after dinner and some more drinks, I cranked the car, the accelerator stuck, and I went smashing into the brick wall."

"Anybody hurt?" I asked.

"No," Rigsby replied, "but the car was totaled."

"What did you do then?"

"Well, my associates suggested I push the car away from the wall, call the police, and tell them that while I was in the restaurant, my car was smashed and whoever did it drove away."

"Did the scheme work?" I inquired.

"I think the police were really going for my story," said Rigsby, "until they found the brick in the grillwork of the car."

"Did they book you?" I went on.

"For being drunk, of course," Rigsby explained, "and also for carrying a concealed weapon."

"A concealed weapon?"

"You're not going to believe this: I had ordered a steak for dinner, but I couldn't eat it all. So I asked for a doggie bag. I also thought of the fact that if I was going to eat the rest of my steak later in my room, I would need a knife.

"When nobody was looking, I slipped my knife into my inside coat pocket. I tried to explain that to the officers, but they didn't believe me, especially since I had been so intent on taking the knife, I had forgotten the doggie bag with the rest of my steak in it."

His associates, Rigsby said, finally were able to obtain his release in the wee hours of the morning. He took a taxi back to his hotel.

"I was still drunk," he said, "so I checked in again. It was the next morning before I discovered I had two keys and two rooms. I should never have drunk those last six tequila shooters."

The selection committee (me) already is looking for candidates for next year's award. If you think you or somebody you know qualifies, enter soon. Remember, the bigger the fool you made of yourself, the better chance you have to win.

"I'll drink to that," said Rigsby, whose latest escapade was getting soused and losing his rental car.

"I parked it somewhere in the Midwest," he explained. "I just can't remember which state."

Cooter Brown, rest his soul, would have been proud.

Journalism Lesson

The $1.6 million libel judgment handed down against the *National Enquirer* in favor of entertainer Carol Burnett may not have sounded like earth-shaking news to most of the nation, but to those of us in the rumor and innuendo business, it was a landmark decision.

Such a thing could lead to the unspeakable: columnists, like yours truly, might have to start dealing in facts. Most of us became columnists because gathering facts is hard work and facts will ruin a good story quicker than anything.

Most readers, I have found, know little about how a newspaper works. In order to show you just how much trouble this Carol Burnett thing could cause, let me give you a little short course in print journalism that you won't get on "Lou Grant."

First, there is the "legitimate" press. Newspapers in big towns like Atlanta, Washington and Boston and New York and Chicago, and newspapers in little towns like Paducah and Moline and Valdosta are "legitimate" newspapers.

That means they actually pay "reporters" to go out and gather "facts." Their columnists are the only ones who can just make stuff up.

(There is an exception to every rule, of course, as in the case this week of the *Washington Post* reporter who won a Pulitzer for a figment of her imagination. Too bad the *Post* editors never noticed her potential as a columnist.)

On the other hand, there is the "illegitimate" press, like the *National Enquirer* and other such newspapers one usually can purchase in supermarkets. Reporters, columnists, the publisher— EVERYBODY—on these newspapers writes gossip, trash, and totally unfounded rumors like Secretary of State Alexander Haig is really a robot and Richard Nixon has the controls.

So they stick it to the *National Enquirer* today. Tomorrow, it could be the "legitimate" press they come after, and who they will come after first are stiffs like me who have to test our imaginations day after day. Anybody can report the "facts."

Prominent local businessman Ernest T. Broomthistle, of Broomthistle and Farkle, was fined $10 in City Traffic Court today for an illegal lane change on Oak Street.

Who wants to read dull garbage like that? Any columnist worth his salt could do a lot more with ol' Broomthistle. Stand back and watch me work:

"So the cops have finally nabbed ol' Ernie 'Big E' Broomthistle, the big-biz bigwig of Broomthistle and Farkle, local manufacturer of women's hosiery, and, according to certain sources, a few other unmentionable garments that are listed only in a 'special' catalog, not readily available to the general public.

"The charge against Broomthistle, who always wears sunglasses and drives a big black car, was 'illegal lane change.' Don't make me laugh. He was stopped on Oak Street, only five blocks from the Three Moons Lounge. What does that tell you?

"A little checking also indicated Broomthistle's partner, Milburn Farkle, lives on Oak Street with his wife, Mona (alias Boom-Boom), former Miss Oklahoma City Rodeo, 1959. Mr. Farkle, it seems, was out of town on business the day his partner and alleged best friend, Broomthistle, was caught weaving all over the road just a few blocks up from where his wife was home all alone, probably wearing some of those unmentionable garments from the 'special catalog.'

"The judge who handed down the paltry $10 fine against Broomthistle was Judge Garvin Pendergrass, incidentally. Some interesting connections between Broomthistle and Pendergrass also have been uncovered.

"Pendergrass, for instance, is originally from Virginia. Broomthistle is from Delaware. Both states were included in the thirteen original colonies.

"One other thing. Both men are bilingual."

If they ever do come after me like they went after the *National Enquirer*, I hope the jury will remember just one thing: It ain't easy being a genius.

A Word for Insomniacs

Because of my vast knowledge of many subjects, readers write to me and ask all sorts of questions.

Some of the questions aren't very nice. Like, when are you going to leave town? And, how did a creep like you get a job with the newspaper?

However, I do get intelligent, interesting questions, and one that came recently was quite intriguing. The question had to do with insomnia, which millions of Americans, including myself, suffer in varying degrees.

The question was: "Dear Mr. Grizzard, I have insomnia. I lie awake all night long in my bed and hear strange noises which make me very nervous and, of course, unable to sleep. What are these noises and are they really nothing to worry about?"

The letter was signed. "Scared Silly, Tupelo, Mississippi."

I am glad you wrote to me, Scared Silly, and I hope I can help. From childhood, we all are frightened of "things that go bump in the night." Some of us grow out of this fear, others do not.

You obviously haven't grown out of this fear, and neither have I. For years I have suffered from insomnia because I know "something" is out there in the dark. I can hear "it" creaking and crawling and coming to get me.

I especially hear these noises when I have watched the Friday Night Horror Double Feature or when I had lots of garlic for dinner.

I am sorry I can't allay your fears, Scared Silly, but I still may be able to offer some assistance by identifying the noises you may be hearing and explaining what they mean.

Incidentally, do not read this while you are alone or where something can sneak up behind you.

● CREEEEEAK! This is a sound commonly heard in the night by insomniacs and other chickens. It probably is nothing. Then, again, it could be the sound of one of your doors slowly being pushed open by an escapee from a local mental institution who inspired the movie *The Texas Chainsaw Massacre*.

● BLIP! BLIP! BLIP! Probably nothing more than a dripping faucet. But what if it were something else? What if it were the sound of blood slowly dripping onto the floor? Your floor. The floor in the next room. A wounded, mad-dog killer has escaped from the authorities and is looking for another victim. Either that, or Dracula has come to suck the blood from your neck. I'll take my chances with the mad-dog killer.

• BLAM! I hear that sound all the time. It's nothing, I tell myself. A book fell off a table. It's the ice maker in the refrigerator. The wind blew one of the shutters against the side of the house. Burglars are working their way to the bedroom to finish off any possible witnesses. Demons, like the kind that got Linda Blair, are throwing my den furniture around. Killer bees are building their hive in the attic.

• WHOOOOOSH! That's nothing. That's just somebody flushing a toilet. But you are alone in the house.

• THUUUUMP! Anybody who has ever been awake at night knows this one. You always hear it as you are just about to doze off. You awaken and you lie there, listening for another sound. You are afraid to move. If you move, "it" will know where you are and "it" will find you. If you should hear a second THUUUUMP, don't even bother to scream.

I hope this helps, Scared Silly, and be sure to write me again if there is anything else I can do. Incidentally, before you go to bed tonight, there is one last thing I should mention.

"It" was last seen near Tupelo, Mississippi. Sweet dreams.

True Grits

I was hoping that four years of Georgian Jimmy Carter in the White House would finally clear up the matter of grits. Grits have been so terribly misunderstood by people who are from parts of the country other than the South.

But, alas, Georgia's Jimmy is only a few weeks from departing Washington in favor of Californian Ronald Reagan, who wouldn't know grits from granola, and I fear grits will never cross the gap that has left so many yet unaware of the history and many uses of one of America's most interesting foods.

As one of the nation's leading experts on grits (my mother served them every morning for breakfast), all I can do is try to light the way for those still blinded by prejudice and fear.

Grits won't bite you. Grits taste good and they're good for you. Just sit back and relax and put yourself in my hands and let go. "DISCOVERING GRITS: GRIZZARD'S GUIDE TO A SOUTHERN DELICACY FOR FOLKS FROM NEW JERSEY AND PLACES LIKE THAT":

● The origin of grits:

Cherokee Indians, native to the Southern region of the United States, first discovered grits trees growing wild during the thirteenth century. Chief Big Bear's squaw, Jemima Big Bear, is said to have been out of oatmeal one day, so she gathered the tiny grits growing from the grits trees and cooked them in water for Chief Big Bear.

After eating the grits, Chief Big Bear ordered his squaw, Jemima, burned at the stake.

Later, however, Southern planter Jim Dandy

found grits taste a lot better if you put salt and pepper and butter on them. Grits really took off in the South after that. Today, grits orchards may be seen from the Carolinas to Florida and west to Louisiana.

At some orchards, tourists may "pick their own grits." If you decide to give it a try, make certain each grit you pick is ripe and firm. Raw grits tend to stick to the roof of your mouth and have been known to choke even large goats.

● How grits got their name:

From the Cherokee word, *greyette*, which means "corn pebbles." The Cherokee thought grits were tiny versions of corn. They even tried to make bread from grits, which brought about another big run on squaw-burning.

● What does the word "hominy" mean?

It is Southern for "blended voices," as in, "That quartet sure has nice hominy, don't it?"

● How to prepare grits:

First, go out to your grits tree and pick a peck of grits. Wash, then allow to soak in warm buttermilk for an hour. Add two tablespoons Jack Daniel (Black Label) Tennessee sippin' whiskey and one cup branch water.

Stir, bake at 450 for approximately one hour. Cover with sawmill gravy, add butter, than salt and pepper to taste. Cheese (Kraft American) optional.

Must be served hot. Cold grits tend to get gummy. You wouldn't serve cold, gummy grits to communist sympathizers from New York.

● What are some other uses for grits?

Patching blow-outs. Snake bite. Bathroom calking. In some parts of the South it is even believed grits will grow hair. This is doubtful. Grits do make a delightful party punch, however. Just add more Jack Daniel.

● How can I order my grits tree?

By sending $38.95 for each tree desired to "Grits-a-Grow-Grow," in care of me. Add $15 if you want to take advantage of our special offer for our handy "Grit-Picker," which will save time and wear and tear on your hands when you go out to gather your grits off your new grits tree.

● What else may I order from "Grits-a-Grow-Grow"?

A special brochure outlining how you can purchase valuable vacation property at our new Alligator Point resort in Florida and about six zillion copies of Amy Carter's Washington Coloring Book. Order now while they last.

4

ORDINARY PEOPLE

The best stories are true stories, the real stories about real people . . . .

Team Man

The little boy who lives at my house is about to embark upon his first season of organized baseball. He is barely housebroken, but they have something called Tee-ball for youngsters still only a short pop fly from the cradle.

In Tee-ball, there is no pitcher. The ball sits on a tee, perfectly still, to make it easier for the child to swat it.

A golfer probably invented Tee-ball.

Regardless of how easy they make it for kids in Tee-ball, the little boy who lives at my house is going to have some problems.

First, he doesn't understand the basics of the game of baseball. I thought boy-children were born with the knowledge of how to run the bases, as in you run to first first.

Not so. When he tried out for his team, his coach asked him to run the bases.

He ran to second first, to third second, to home third, and then slid into first last.

Actually, it wasn't a slide. It was more of a *crawl*.

Later, I asked the little boy why he crawled on his stomach into first base.

He said, "That's the way baseball players do it because they don't want anybody to see them sneaking into the base."

Oh.

The biggest problem he is going to have, however, is with his thumb-sucking.

Now, let's go over thumb-sucking for a moment.

There is nothing wrong with it. Sucking one's thumb does not make one a bad person.

It is just a habit, a way children relax and relieve tension. Adults have double martinis, kids have thumb-sucking.

If double martinis were suddenly taken away from them, a lot of adults probably would suck their thumbs.

I am certain the little boy eventually will dispense with sucking his thumb, but likely not before his first game of Tee-ball and that's the big trouble here.

I had never thought of this before, but after going out into the yard and tossing a few balls around with the little boy to get him ready for the season, I realized how hard it is to play baseball and suck your thumb at the same time.

Consider: The child is a lefty. He bats, throws, and sucks left.

So, he's playing the outfield and a long fly ball is hit in his direction. The winning run is at third, one out. The runner will try to tag and come home.

The little boy runs for the ball, which is no easy task with a thumb in your mouth. He catches it, but before he can make his throw to the plate, he must remove his thumb from his mouth, hoping the rest of his throwing hand will follow.

The split second he loses with all that wasted motion allows the winning run to score. He is the goat of the game.

I tried to make that point to him.

"You don't want to let the rest of the Cardinals down, do you?" I asked him, appealing to his conscience.

"No," he replied. "I'll try to remember not to suck my thumb when there is anybody on base."

At least the kid's a team man, thumb in or thumb out.

Learning a Lesson

WASHINGTON, D.C.—The kid was twelve, maybe thirteen, and he had sad eyes and a look about him that said he wanted to cry.

But he wouldn't cry, because streetwise kids from the tough neighborhoods are cried out by his age.

He was standing at the entrance to Washington's bustling Union Station, hiding, sort of, behind one of the giant pillars.

All about him were travelers, coming and going, and why he picked me, I don't know. This taxi had dropped me off with my bags. My train would leave in fifteen minutes.

"Can I carry your bags to the train, mister?" the kid asked.

I travel a great deal by train. The way you get your bags down to the train is you find a dying breed called a "redcap," and he puts your bags on the train, and then you pay him maybe two dollars for the service.

Sometimes you can find a redcap. Sometimes you can't. I looked around. I didn't see a redcap. I had more bags than I could handle. Time was running out on me.

I looked at the kid again. Maybe this is some kind of new sting, I thought. The kid takes my bags and when I turn my head for a moment, he is gone, and so are my bags.

But not this kid. Don't ask me how I knew that, I just knew that. Listen, I said to myself, at least he's trying to *work*. He could be out trying to break into a house or into somebody's car.

So just as I was about to turn over my bags to the kid, up walks a redcap.

"Get out of here, kid!" he shouts, and the kid recoils at first, and then makes a stand of it.

"I ain't doin' nothin' wrong," the kids says to the redcap, and then they go one-on-one.

"You got no business out here!"

"I'm just tryin' to make a coupla dollars. What's wrong with that, man?"

"Ain't nothin' wrong with that, except it's my two dollars you tryin' to make."

"I got a right to work out here, too."

"You ain't got no kind of right to work out here. You too young, for one thing."

"I ain't too young."

"The hell you ain't. And you ain't paid no union dues, either, man."

At this point, the kid is stymied. Also, imagine my predicament. Now, my train is leaving in ten minutes, and I'm still standing outside the station.

A station security guard appears out of the air.

"What's the problem?" he asks the redcap.

"Stupid kid's out here hustling my bags, that's the problem," the redcap answers.

Eight minutes to go until train time.

"Don't you know you have to be hired before you can go to work out here?" the security guard asks the kid.

"I just wanted to make a coupla dollars. What's wrong with that, man?" repeats the kid.

"It just don't work that way, son," says the security guard, and by now the redcap has my bags on his cart and he is wheeling them to my train, which I barely will make.

I left the kid with the security guard.

As I handed the two dollars to the redcap for

putting my bags onto the train, he said to me, "Don't worry about that kid. He'll learn soon enough. It's every man for himself out here."

Kids. It just takes them a while to catch on, that's all.

Good News

Earl Sheriff, sixty-eight, is custodian at the little high school in the village of Fredericktown, Ohio, which is near Columbus.

You ought to hear them talk about "Mr. Sheriff" around the school.

"He's the sweetest, kindest, most helpful man I've ever known," one of the teachers was saying. "We couldn't get along without him."

Still, nobody knew much about Earl Sheriff's background until one day when some of the students, who were in the midst of a course called U.S. Wars, casually asked the custodian if he knew anything about WW II, the Big One.

Earl Sheriff knew quite a bit. He had lived through it, as a matter of fact, and the students asked him to come and lecture the class.

So here is the school custodian lecturing in the classroom, and Sgt. Earl Sheriff talked about how he had served as a light machine-gun section leader and how he had hit Utah Beach with the 121st Infantry as part of the first replacement unit in after D-Day.

He also mentioned fighting through the hedgerow country of France and into the Hurtgen Forest. And he brought along his Purple Heart—he was wounded three times—and his Silver Star and his Medal of Luxembourg.

"The light machine guns went ahead of the infantry," Earl Sheriff told the students. "We were up there where we could look the Germans in the eyes. It was hell, but we had a job to do, and we did it—and a lot of good boys got killed."

An old soldier remembers, and today's high school students, ages fifteen through seventeen, listen to stories of a fabled time when Americans went to war wearing white hats, and "technical problems" didn't scrub missions. Somebody fixed the machine and the fight went on.

Ancient history, in other words.

When Earl Sheriff finished his lecture, one of the students asked him if he ever saw any of the men he had fought beside.

The custodian said there was an annual reunion of the 121st, but he had never been able to attend.

"Never could get time off from work," he said. Another problem is that his wife is an invalid.

I wondered about those students. Did they really care today how we gave Hitler hell, and what the cost of it was? Have we been on a losing streak so long they could not look at the old man in front of them and sense his pride for having a job to do, and for having done it?

Get the picture here. As the students' teacher put it, "This is still middle America. This is mostly a farm community. These are good kids. They care."

They do. I'll keep this short. What the students did was canvass the school and ask for donations. They raised $250, and they gave it to Earl Sheriff for a round-trip airplane ticket to Macon, Georgia, this week.

There he will attend the reunion of the 121st Infantry Regiment for the first time.

"Seeing all those fellows again," he said, "was always a dream of mine. Now it is coming true."

A group of high school students in 1980 have dug deep into their pockets for an old soldier who fought with our last winner.

You're always clamoring for "good" news out there. This should be a gracious dose.

Forgotten Hero

I heard him tell the story so many times.

He and his men were camped in some god-forsaken place in Korea. The Chinese had just entered the war in November. The year was 1950.

"They caught us completely by surprise," he

said. "I looked up at this hill and every gook on earth was coming over it."

War was nothing new to him. He had fought his way through France, leading nineteen-year-olds, six years earlier.

"Fighting Germans," he would explain, "was one thing, but fighting these crazy people was something else. German soldiers were intelligent, they thought like Americans. You could figure out their next move.

"These people, the Chinese, were nuts. They didn't value human life. You'd kill one and ten more would come over that hill to take his place." His company was being annihilated. He was sure he would die. He had a wife and a kid back home.

"About thirty of us, the last ones left, dug a pit and held them off for hours," he would go on. "But they finally pitched a mortar right in the middle of the pit. It took off the head of this kid. I'll never forget seeing that. The chaplain got it, too.

"There was so much smoke and noise, I didn't know if anybody else around me was alive. I pulled some bodies over me and prayed they wouldn't notice me."

Maybe it was the prayers. The enemy didn't notice him. He waited under the bodies for hours, afraid to bat an eye, afraid to move for fear of being discovered.

Finally, he stood up. There was total silence around him, a sea of dead. He looked around in the pit. He found a young soldier still breathing. He poured water out of his canteen onto the young soldier's face. He came around.

"I knew he was hurt, but I had to move him," he explained. He carried the soldier as he wandered into the night. When he became so tired he couldn't go another inch, he sat down under a tree and propped the soldier against the tree next to him.

He slept. Sometime in the night, his only companion died.

He continued to wander, now alone, through the next morning. It was a friendly North Korean soldier, who had been forced into duty and was hiding himself, who saw him and befriended him and saved the man's life.

He took the American back to where his family was living in a lean-to at the base of a mountain. He put the American in a hole and covered the hole with boards and straw. Each day for six weeks, he would emerge from his own hiding place to bring the American rice in the hole. The American could hear enemy troop movement around him.

Water seeped into the hole, but the American didn't dare come out for fear of being discovered. His feet froze. When it was finally safe to travel, he said his steps were like "walking on two basketballs."

The friendly soldier eventually led him back to the American lines. The Army notified the man's family that he was no longer missing in action. After a hospital stay in Pearl Harbor, he was allowed to come home.

He had distinguished himself. He had fought two wars for his country. He had a head full of shrapnel, two bullet holes in his hip, and he wouldn't be able to sleep without first emptying a bottle of amber medicine.

His wife and son and his mother-in-law met him at the train when he arrived home. A local newspaper reporter showed up, too.

But there was no band, no parade, no well wishes, nor a message from his commander-in-chief. He never complained, of course, but later there was little, if any, rehabilitation, either. He never really made it back from that pit in Korea from under the bodies of those dead friends.

His feet bled every day. He died a drunk and a pauper.

We didn't do anything wrong welcoming home the former hostages from Iran. They deserved every yellow ribbon, every hand held out toward them.

But a lot of heroes who preceded them went virtually unnoticed, and for one in particular, I've felt a tinge of bitterness lately. I demand at least that.

Townsend

Jim Townsend died soon after I wrote the following piece. I'm convinced he is presently in heaven,

> *trying to con Hemingway and Voltaire into doing*
> *something for the new magazine he's starting.*

This will probably read like a book review, but it's not. It's a story about a friend of mine who recently had a book published, a special friend more people genuinely love than just about anybody else I know.

His name is Townsend.

Yeah, he's got a first name, "James," and a middle initial, "L.," but you don't need any of those. He is "Townsend," always "Townsend," forever "Townsend."

His book is *Dear Heart* (Peachtree Publishers), and in his book Townsend takes you from Lanett, Alabama, his hometown, to any number of magic places, with numerous stops in Atlanta, a city he describes as the best city in America for "rearing a family, living in safety, and moving around without unreasonable delay."

One of the reasons so many people love Townsend so much is because he would be optimistic with all four engines out and the tail section on fire, flying through a hurricane.

Townsend, among other things, founded *Atlanta Magazine*. He edited it and nursed it, and he did the same in Cincinnati and in New Orleans and you name the town, chances are Townsend put his genius to work there at some point.

But Atlanta, how the man loves Atlanta.

In the introduction to *Dear Heart*, fellow author and friend Pat Conroy says of Townsend and what he's meant to this city:

"Atlanta, forgetful city, feisty and brawling and on the go, has not yet honored Jim Townsend, has not paused to thank the man, has not slowed down for one single act of gratitude and appreciation to the man who helped to invent the image of Atlanta.

"But when the history of Atlanta is written, and when they talk about who created the soul of this city, they will have to deal with the brilliant, mercurial, contradictory, and infinitely complex figure of Jim Townsend."

I first met Townsend in a bar. When you met Townsend a few years back, you always met him in a bar.

"Grizzard," he said to me. "I've got a story only you can do." Townsend said that to all the writers.

You didn't always get paid. Lee Walburn, now editor-in-chief of *Atlanta Weekly*, explains on the back of Townsend's new book why that never really bothered you as much as it probably should have:

"Townsend is a lovable old basset hound of an editor whose eloquent cajolery has charmed a million words from hundreds of writers—sometimes for pay, sometimes for promises. The sharing of this collection from his own jewel bag of words pays all debts."

Townsend finally whipped his boozing problem. Now he's got another bear to fight. Cancer.

Still, he's down almost every day on the seventh floor at 72 Marietta Street where *Atlanta Weekly* comes together. He edits. He writes notes. Townsend is the most eloquent note-writer who ever doodled across a scratch pad.

His book sings. There are tent revivals, twenty-fifth anniversary parties at ice cream parlors, and he explains what a "gradualist" is, and you meet H.L. Hunt and Count Alexis de Sakhnoffsky, and there is a piece about Townsend's daddy who was sharecropping cotton in West Georgia when McKinley was shot down in Buffalo.

I just want to say one more thing, and I want to say it directly to Townsend:

I read your book in one easy sitting, and I won't be satisfied until I've read more. You're beautiful, dear heart. Just beautiful.

No Easy Way Out

We aren't, well, close, but we've had a few high times together, enough to keep us reminiscing for a couple of hours at least before we have to start telling the same stories over again.

So I was shocked when I heard the news. This man, a young man, put a .38-caliber pistol to his head. And pulled the trigger.

Say you are just trying to get somebody's

attention or sympathy. You take a few pills and wind up getting your stomach pumped out in the hospital.

I'm no shrink, but I know that if you put a pistol to your head and pull the trigger, you are serious about leaving us.

It's like the man's attorney said later: "Imagine his surprise when he woke up and found out he wasn't in the Promised Land after all. He was right back here with the rest of us."

Yeah, he lived. Barely. They were already talking about where to send the remains.

I went to see him in the hospital the other night. I'm not going to mention his name. He's had enough bad publicity in his life already, and there are two children who carry his name.

"You look awful," I said to him.

"Can you believe this?" he laughed. His spirits were surprisingly high. "The last thing in the world I try to do, and I louse it up."

He spared no details.

I already knew about his divorce. Then he ran afoul of the law. Nothing big-time, but enough to bring the heat close enough to feel it.

Then, there was the lady. Stop me if you've heard this one before.

"I thought she was really special," he said.

"They've got that way of fooling us sometimes," I said.

"I just fell apart," he said. "All I could think of was I wanted out. I wanted my ticket punched."

"So what did you do, uh, wrong?" I asked. He

held a finger of his right hand to his head and explained to me what the doctors had explained to him.

"They said I held the gun at an angle, so the bullet went through my right eye and out above my left eye. They said most people who shoot themselves in the head hold the gun straight, and it blows their brains out."

Above his left eye was the hole where the bullet left his head. He has lost his right eye. I made some crack about women thinking eyepatches are sexy. He is lucky he isn't blind.

I had to ask. I had to ask what it felt like to nearly die. You've read all those stories of what people saw and felt before they miraculously escaped death's clutches.

"I don't remember anything," he said. "There was a thud in my head after I pulled the trigger, and then, two days later, I woke up and I didn't know if I was in heaven or hell. I just knew I had an awful headache and there were tubes all over me."

There was something else I had to ask. I wanted to know if he was happy he had missed the obit page after all his efforts to make it there.

"I tried to get out, and I didn't make it," he answered.

He is no manner of a poet, and I have never seen sensitivity in him before. But he had something he wanted me to read. On a yellow sheet he had scribbled out the following words:

I am an incurable romantic. I believe in hopes, dreams, and decency. I believe in love, tenderness, kindness, and family. I believe in mankind.

But I must never let my happiness depend entirely on another person's thoughts, whims, or demands. Nor can I forget the value of honesty, the harshness at times of reality, and warmth of life itself, nor the need for love.

Nice thoughts, I got up to leave.

"If you write something in the paper about this," said the man, "will you do me one favor?"

"Sure. What?"

"Tell anybody who's thinking of doing what I did not to do it. It's not the easy way out after all."

Dark Eyes

It's an old story. She was seventeen at the time. She's more than twice that now, but still dark-eyed and beautiful. The first time I saw her, half of my life ago, she nearly took my breath.

It was a small town in the hills, and her mother taught in the little high school. Her father split when she was a baby. Her mother never remarried. There were no more children.

Her mother raised her on grace and good manners.

"Mama," she would say, laughing, "Mama always told me to act like she was looking over my shoulder. I always knew that, somehow, she was."

The child grew to be a beauty, and also a scholar. Besides that, she sang in church and visited the old people.

The boys flocked around her and vied for even her slightest attention. Those were simpler times.

She conquered high school in a matter of days. Cheerleader, clubs, a dozen handsome fellows already left in her wake by her junior year.

She was perfect. Life was perfect. Nothing could go wrong.

Something went wrong. Forget about a drug, booze, or sex angle here, however. This was the early sixties, small town, and Homecoming Night at the high school stadium.

She was one of the finalists, and she would win, of course, because she was the most popular girl in school. The homecoming queen would be chosen by ballot of the student body, the results to be announced at half time.

She was dazzling that night, a girl-child on the fine edge of womanhood.

The results were announced. She won. Her mother beamed; she had done her best under some tough circumstances.

There was another family in the town that was THE family in town. If you worked in town, normally you worked for THE family. They lived in the big house with shade trees framing the drive up to the front door.

And there was a daughter in the family, too, the same age as dark-eyes, and she was a member of the Homecoming Court that night, too.

When the name of the queen was announced, the mother of the loser stormed school officials and demanded that the ballots be recounted. Don't forget, THE family gave money for the new gymnasium and bought uniforms for the band.

The ballots were recounted. At the end of the game, there was a simple announcement. There had been a mistake. There was a new homecoming queen.

They made dark-eyes give back her crown and her roses.

"I thought I would die," she said. "And I think I would have if it hadn't been for Mama. The embarrassment was incredible. Mama said, 'Go back to school, face whatever comes. If you run from this, it could change your entire life.' "

She didn't run. She went back to school. And when it was her time, she caught a bus out of town and never looked back.

We met again by chance the other day. I didn't mention the story, and neither did she. She's been a resounding success. The lady has guts.

I do wish I knew whatever happened to Miss Homecoming, though. I hope she got fat.

5

EATING LIVER
AND OTHER SINS

---

*One thing that has always puzzled me: everytime I
write a column in which I mention God, at least five
people write me a letter and threaten to kill me....*

Preacher Jokes

We had the minister over for dinner the other evening, and I think this all is a part of my wife's grand plans to civilize me. Next, she probably will want me to start sleeping in pajamas. Cowboys don't sleep in pajamas, but how could a woman know that?

Anyway, back to the minister coming to dinner. I had all sorts of rules I was to follow:

● You can have a beer or two, she said, but don't get out of your mind and start wanting to sing Maurice Williams and the Zodiacs songs like you do when it's just a regular party with your weirdo friends.

● And above all, don't tell any of your preacher jokes.

My wife was very emphatic about that last rule because she knows I enjoy telling jokes about preachers.

I don't know how I got started collecting jokes about ministers, but I have what must be hundreds in my repertoire, most of which are entirely within the bounds of good taste. You even can tell them at a Rotary Club luncheon.

I have short preacher jokes:

How do you tell the difference between a Northern Baptist preacher and a Southern Baptist preacher?

A Northern Baptist preacher will tell you there ain't no hell. A Southern Baptist preacher will tell you, The hell there ain't!

(For what they pay you to tell jokes at a Rotary Club luncheon, it does just fine.)

I also have long preacher jokes:

Once there was this small town where the Methodist preacher and the Baptist preacher, both of whom were quite young, rode bicycles. One Sunday morning the Methodist preacher was riding his bicycle to church and he spotted the Baptist preacher, who was on foot.

"Where is your bicycle, brother?" the Methodist preacher asked.

"My heart is heavy," replied the Baptist preacher, "I think a member of my congregation has stolen it."

The Methodist preacher was appalled. "I think I can help you," he said. "When you're in the pulpit this morning, preach on the Ten Commandments. And when you come to 'Thou Shalt Not Steal,' you bear down on it, and maybe the person who stole your bicycle will get the message and be moved to return it to you."

The Baptist preacher said he would try his colleague's suggestion. Two weeks later they met again. Sure enough, the Baptist preacher had his bicycle back.

"I see my plan worked," the Methodist preacher said.

"Not exactly," said the Baptist preacher. "I did preach on the Ten Commandments, but when I got to 'Thou Shalt Not Commit Adultery,' I remembered where I left my bicycle."

That was the specific joke my wife had in mind when she told me not to tell our minister any of my preacher stories.

It was a marvelous dinner party. Just before we called it a night, the minister turned to me and said, "Hey, did you hear about the preacher who ran off with all the church's money and went to Las Vegas?"

I hadn't heard.

"Part of the money he gambled away. Part of it he spent on booze. Part of if he spent on wild women. The rest of it, he just squandered."

Amen, brother.

The Lord's Collection Agent

Rose Emmett, who loved the Lord and didn't mind sharing her meager fixed income with him, received a certified letter a couple of weeks ago in Atlanta from none other than Oral and Evelyn Roberts.

Oral Roberts, of course, is the famous evangelist and faith healer. Evelyn is his wife.

"Dear Sister Emmett," the letter began. "Evelyn and I have knelt and prayed over every word in this letter before dropping it to you."

I probably don't have to tell you what the letter was about, but, for the record, let's go over it again.

Out in Tulsa, Oral Roberts is busy trying to raise money for something called the "City of Faith." What Oral Roberts wants to do is build a sixty-floor hospital complex, which would be the tallest building in Tulsa, as a "testimony to the glory of God."

Oral Roberts's "City of Faith" project has run into problems lately. First, his "partners," donors offering funds for the building, have been a little slow with their contributions. Also, a Tulsa group headed by a local physician has openly opposed Roberts' project as unneeded in the area.

In another fund-raising letter recently, Roberts came up with a real zinger. He says that May 25, he spoke to Jesus and Jesus said he would speak to Oral Roberts's "partners" to assure that the project will be completed.

In his vision, incidentally, Roberts said Jesus appeared as 900 feet tall.

Rose Emmett was one of Oral Roberts's "partners" who had been a little slow in contributing lately. That apparently is what prompted Oral and Evelyn to send her the certified letter.

Mrs. Emmett's daughter sent me the letter. I will quote from parts of it:

"The (City of Faith) construction is standing right outside my window.... The enemy is on an all-out attack, and we are facing one of the largest emergencies we have ever faced. Can you imagine what the enemies of this ministry would say if Oral Roberts failed?

"This letter you are now holding can be the greatest letter you have ever held. It can be a door to not only the answer to this emergency we are facing, but also the miracle that you need.

"...God spoke to my heart to present this emergency to you like this: If you saw a beautiful home or an automobile for sale for $100, you would be foolish not to buy it (even if you had to borrow the $100 and pay it back in small monthly payments.)

"This emergency we are facing is more than just a house, or automobile. It is a crisis for God. If we do not meet it, this ministry will suffer as never before....

"Remember," the letter closed, "if you do not have the $100, we will be praying here in Tulsa that God will lead you, as He did Evelyn and me, to where you can get it."

There was also a P.S., one last plea from Oral Roberts:

"I am going to cancel my plans and wait right

here on this (enclosed) envelope from you....Oral Roberts is here praying...waiting...watching the mail for the answer from you concerning this emergency for God's work!!!"

You can stop "praying...waiting...watching" now, Oral. You can also stop counting on Rose Emmett to stroll down to her friendly finance company to pick up the hundred she could have so easily paid back in small monthly payments.

Your letter arrived three months too late. Back in July, Mrs. Rose Emmett, eighty-five, died of a brain tumor in the nursing home where your certified letter was mailed.

"Mrs. Emmett had sent him money before," said her son-in-law. "That's how they knew where to find her. The letter made me boil. Imagine asking an elderly lady like that on a fixed income to go out and borrow the money to give him if she didn't have it."

Just imagine.

The Lord works in mysterious ways, but when it comes to downright chicanery, some of his self-appointed "crusaders"—not mentioning any names—wrote the book.

Interviewing Reverend Falwell

For weeks, this column attempted through legitimate means to reach the Rev. Jerry Falwell, head of the Moral Majority, to discuss his recent "interview" with *Penthouse* magazine.

As most everyone knows, Reverend Falwell claims he was tricked and was not aware that the interview he gave would appear in *Penthouse*, a publication that involves itself with frontal nudity and bad words, and even allows advertisements of liquor.

My attempts to reach Reverend Falwell went for naught, however.

"Does your newspaper print advertisements for moving pictures?" I was asked by one of Reverend Falwell's press aides.

"Of course," I said.

"Even those rated R and X?" the aide asked.

"Those are especially popular with our readers," I answered.

"Then you may NOT interview Reverend Falwell," said the aide, hanging up the phone.

I refuse to be put off that easily. The public has a right to know. Behind these glasses and this frail, unassuming exterior beats the heart of a lion in pursuit of his prey.

I am proud to announce I have just returned from Falwell's Lynchburg, Virginia, headquarters and I got my interview, despite the odds against me.

I disguised myself as a duck.

"Your name?" I was asked at the reception desk.

"Chuck," I said.

"A Mr. Chuck Duck to see Reverend Falwell," the receptionist called to Falwell's secretary.

"Go right in, Mr. Duck," said the receptionist.

"What is the purpose of your visit?" the secretary asked.

"I would like to interview Reverend Falwell," I said.

"And whom do you represent?" she continued.

"Duck Daily," I said.

"Does your publication involve itself with any sort of lewdity, such as photographs of naked bodies?"

"An occasional graceful swan in a wading pool," I answered, "but nothing graphic. Mostly, it's just news of interest to ducks."

"Such as?" the secretary persisted.

"Oh, what to do when you get a cold in your quacker, or how to react if your son or daughter starts dating a duckbill platypus."

"I thought you said there was no lewdity in your publication," the secretary said.

"We keep it clean," I said. "We don't even spell out the word 'sex' in our articles. We use the phrase 'you know what.' Last week, for instance, we carried an article titled, 'After Hours Down by the Old Millstream: The You-Know-What Life of a Wild Goose.'"

I could tell I had won the secretary over. She buzzed her boss.

"Reverend Falwell will see you now," she said. I was ushered into the reverend's office. Plush, but not extravagant.

"Chuck Duck of Duck Daily, Reverend Falwell," I said. He was pleasant and open and held steadfastly to his contention that *Penthouse* had hornswoggled him.

"But it won't happen again," he insisted.

As I emerged from his office, a large rabbit sat waiting.

"And whom do you represent, Mr. Rabbit?" asked the secretary.

"*Popular Mechanics*," said the rabbit, winking to me as I waddled out the door.

Out With Sin

Now that the Moral Majority is exercising a great deal of influence upon our government and our society, it should be obvious that sin is out.

During the sixties and seventies, sin definitely was in. Avarice certainly had its moments, but Lust probably was the big sin of that period.

Even women, heretofore believed totally pure, got involved, and women's magazines suddenly were carrying more than recipes for apple strudel.

Lust among women hit an all-time high when a magazine published a centerfold of famous actor Burt Reynolds in the nude.

Maggie Smeltingham, a seventy-seven-year-old spinster from Grove City, Alabama, lusted with such fervor upon seeing Mr. Reynolds' photograph that she swallowed her snuff and had to have her stomach pumped.

"If I met such a man face to face," a local minister said of Mr. Reynolds, "I don't know what word I could use to describe him."

"After I caught my breath," said Maggie Smeltingham, "I would call him, 'Sugar Pie.'"

Now that sin is out, many citizens may have questions concerning exactly what is a sin and what isn't. To help make such distinctions, I contacted my local Moral Majority precinct captain, the Rev. LeRoy "Lucky" Fandango.

The Reverend Fandango is a former professional wrestler who was converted while his head was being rammed into a ring post by his opponent, the Masked Onion No. 2.

"Sin," said Fandango, "is very simple to identify. Just ask these three simple questions:

"1. Is it fun?

"2. Does it feel good?

"3. Is it fattening?

"If you answered 'yes' to any of those questions, you can just bet your boots it's a sin."

"Bet your boots?" I asked.

"Poor choice of words," said Fandango. "Betting, or gambling, offers a certain amount of thrill and excitement, so you can forget it."

I asked Fandango for some more specific examples of sin.

"Gum-chewing, for one," he answered.

"Gum-chewing is a sin?"

"Not in itself," said the Reverend, "but for where it can lead.

"A person starts chewing gum, and the next thing you know, he will go to Lifesavers. After Lifesavers come soft drinks, then booze, and then shooting pool and smoking and cursing and reading filthy magazines."

Moral Majority, of course, has its list of "no-no" magazines. I asked Fandango to mention a few.

"*Playboy*," he said. I expected that. "And *Hustler* and *Penthouse* and the swimsuit issue of *Sports Illustrated* and *National Geographic*."

National Geographic is a sinful magazine?

"Sections on thatch huts in Ireland are fine," said the Reverend Fandango, "but be sure to stay away from anything having to do with tribal rites or lion hunts."

No drinking, no smoking, no lusting at pictures in magazines. So what does the Moral Majority recommend we do for leisure activities?

"There are lots of possibilities," Fandango explained. "Quiet meditation can be a real hoot once you get into it, and prayer-group softball games are okay, as long as nobody wears short pants. The Rev. Jerry Falwell Coloring Book is available on order, and have you ever just sat and watched milk curdle?"

"Might as well," I answered. "Can't dance."

"Dance?" The Reverend Fandango recoiled in horror. "Don't even say the word!"

Saying Grace

The five-year-old boy who lives in my house is learning to say the blessing.

"LET ME SAY THE BLESSING!" he bellows as we sit down to the table.

"GOD IS GOOD!

"GOD IS NEAT!

"LET US THANK HIM!

"FOR ALL WE CAN EAT!

"YEA, GOD!"

My stepson is the only person I know who prays in a primal scream. Not only does God get the message, but so does everybody else within six blocks of our kitchen.

The "Yea, God" blessing is his favorite because it is more a cheer than a blessing, and the child is a human megaphone.

But tolerance is very important here because it is a big deal for a child to learn to say the blessing before the family meal. And it's not that easy, either.

First, you have to think of something to say. I remember when my parents first asked me to say the blessing:

MY FATHER: "Say the blessing, son."

MY MOTHER: "And don't mumble."

ME: "ThankyouGodforthemashedpo—"

MY MOTHER: "You're mumbling."

ME: "—tatoesandthegreenbeansandthepork-chopsandthe—"

MY FATHER: "Amen. That was very good, son, but you don't have to thank God for EVERYTHING on the table."

I wasn't going to mention the rutabagas.

After mastering a nice little blessing your mother thinks is "cute," and doesn't hold your old man away from the grub too long, you move into the "clever" blessings stage.

Everybody knew this one:

"Son, would you please say grace?" your mother would ask, bowing her head.

"Grace," you would reply, howling at your genius.

"Whaack!" would be the sound of the back of your father's hand across your face.

Then there was the old favorite:

> *Good bread,*
> *Good meat,*
> *Good Lord,*
> *Let's eat!*

That was good for the backhand across the face AND getting sent to your room without any dinner.

If you really got brave, you could use this one:

> *Bless the meat,*
> *Damn the skins,*
> *Back your ears,*
> *And cram it in!*

That could get you reform school.

When it came to smart-aleck blessings, my

boyhood friend and idol, Weyman C. Wannamaker, Jr., a great American, had no peer.

His all-time classic was the following:

> *Thank you, Lord, for this meal,*
> *We know you are the giver.*
> *But thank you, Lord, most of all,*
> *That we ain't havin' liver.*

Weyman's father tried to send him to reform school, but the warden was afraid he would be a bad influence on the other "students."

Soon, my stepson will be in the stage of saying "clever" blessings, but I am not going to whack him across the face.

I am going to make him eat liver, smothered in rutabagas.

6

A THIRD LOOK AT
LOVE AND MARRIAGE

I get letters from people who say, "What have you got against women?" What could I possibly have against women? I've married three of them....

The "Love Boat"

Atlanta is blessed with a number of nearby lakes where people go to fish and swim and sail and ski. It is at a marina on one of these lakes where sits what locals have come to call the "love boat" after all these years.

It is a dreadful little houseboat. Somebody painted it white a long time ago, but now the paint is peeling off.

It has a couple of tiny windows that are always closed. A giant padlock keeps would-be intruders out.

Picture this disaster tied amongst expensive, plush houseboats with three and four bedrooms and air conditioning—floating suites.

"You take somebody for a walk along the marina," one of the lake dwellers was telling me, "and they see beautiful boat after beautiful boat, and then they come to the love boat. They all ask. 'What in the world is this thing?'"

For fifteen years, she has appeared at the marina. For fifteen years, every Tuesday and every Thursday, she has arrived in the marina parking lot in an expensive, late-model car.

For fifteen years, every Tuesday and every Thursday, she has gotten out of her car and walked down to the dock, clicking her high heels as she has stridden hurriedly to the love boat.

The locals describe her with awe.

"Beautiful," said one. "An absolutely beautiful woman."

"Stunning," said another.

But she never speaks. For fifteen years, she has never spoken to the others tending to their boats along the dock.

She arrives at the love boat, takes out a key, and unlocks the door. She goes inside. In a few minutes, she emerges and sweeps the small deck.

Rumor has it she occasionally will sweep the deck of the boat in the scantiest of pajamas. This is only a rumor.

Soon after she has finished sweeping and has returned inside the love boat, he arrives. He arrives in a sleek cabin cruiser. He is as handsome as she is beautiful.

He docks his boat, ties up, and goes to the love boat. He doesn't speak to the others, either.

He has his own key. He unlocks the door and goes inside.

Sometimes, it is an hour before the couple

emerges. Sometimes, an hour and a half. But always, they emerge together. She walks with him back up the dock to where his cruiser is tied. They do not speak.

They both step onto the cruiser. He pulls away from the dock and then drops her off at the bank, thus saving her the walk back up the dock.

She goes to her car and drives away. He pulls his cruiser away from the marina and speeds to a nearby bridge that crosses the lake. There, he waits until she drives over the bridge.

As she passes, he stands out on his boat. They wave a final goodbye.

For fifteen years every Tuesday and Thursday, the pattern never changed.

Recently, there has been a change. She is still beautiful, they say. She still drives the nice, expensive car. He still comes dashing up in the cruiser, and they still spend the hour or so in the love boat, and then he waits for one last wave goodbye at the bridge.

"It's sorta sad now, though," said a man who docks near the love boat. "After fifteen years, they've cut out Tuesdays."

It Runs in the Family

The big joke around the office lately goes something like this: "What did you get in the Grizzard pool?"

"The Grizzard what?"

"The Grizzard office pool—how long he'll stay married this time."

That's not very funny, especially when you consider that my secretary, Miss Wanda Fribish, paid a buck to enter and got "eight days."

So I've been married a few times before. Big deal. My Uncle Gaylord, the traveling salesman, recently married his fifth wife, Aunt Mildred, and they are blissfully happy.

Aunt Mildred, incidentally, performs at the Bump 'n' Grind Lounge and Truck Stop near Tulsa, which is where she met Uncle Gaylord one night while she was dancing on his table.

As for me, things are going swimmingly at home. It's been six beautiful weeks, and I had forgotten the difference marriage can make in a person's life.

Hot meals on the table. Back rubs. Clean underwear. And the little woman really seems to enjoy it all.

There will be those detractors, of course, who will continue to insist this heavenly wedlock will never last, no matter what.

But they do not realize how serious I am about making this marriage work. Besides, one more bomb and I'm getting precariously close to double figures.

To prove my rightful intentions, I am about to do something drastic. I am about to reveal publicly the contents of my little black book, the one with all the names of all those delightful lovelies with whom I became acquainted during my single days.

That is a big step for any man, but I am more than willing to take it—and perhaps also provide an opportunity for those lonesome, deprived bachelors in the audience to find the right companion.

Any woman whose name appears on the following list is fair game. My wings, once flapping in the single breeze, have been clipped.

Here goes:

● Marcia Glimstein: waitress. Gets off work at midnight and loves to boogie until dawn. Blonde. Also brunette and redhead, depending on which party ring she's wearing. Shriners welcome.

● Sylvia Mudd: automotive maintenance coordinator. (Works in car wash.) Shining disposition. (Personality of a jar of Turtle Wax.) Bugs on her bumper. (Severe acne problem.) Off Thursdays. (And all rainy days.)

● Shanda Ripplemeyer: stewardess. Sort of. Works air-freight runs in the middle of the night. Wears "Marry Me—Ship Free" T-shirts and sweats a lot. Perfect afternoon date, especially if you need to unload a truck.

● Rhonda de Haven: poet, artist, and checkout girl at Kroger store. Latest works include still life of a cucumber and poem entitled, "Ode to a Frozen Pork Chop." Weird, but cute.

● Mary Jane "Pumpkin" Palmer: cheerleader for professional hockey team. The puck has a higher I.Q., but you ought to see her Zambonis.

● Pauline Gooch: elementary-school teacher. Looking for husband. Wants big family. Could stand to lose a few pounds. Could play linebacker for the Steelers. Fun date if you've never been out with the Goodyear Blimp.

● Natalie Foyt: used car salesperson. Divorcee. Gets dates by running classified ads in personals section. Look under "Clean, 1-owner."

● Tina Marina: crack television news investigative reporter. Won Emmy for in-depth series entitled, "Turning Right on Red: Friend or Foe?" Smart. Witty. Raises chinchillas.

● Alexandria "Bulldog" Mankiewitz: terrorist for local militant women's lib group. Shaves three times a week and then eats the razor blades. Tattoo on left forearm reads, "Born to Raise Hell." Former roller derby star. Idea of a good time is rolling truck drivers.

● Candy Cain: Model, Dancer. Call Sly Fox Escort Agency. Furnishes own film. Uncle Gaylord's fourth wife.

Stand by Your Man

There simply is no way to consider a juicy scandal like the one involving former Rep. John Jenrette of South Carolina and his pretty blonde wife without taking sides.

I'll take his. Rita Jenrette has a big mouth.

Years ago, women who told their husbands'

secrets in public would be stripped of their bridge club memberships and, in cruder societies, flogged. Today they get 10,000 words in *Playboy* magazine and an hour on Donahue.

As if John Jenrette didn't have enough troubles. First, he gets caught in the Abscam web. Then, he loses his bid for re-election and has to resign from the House in disgrace and tears. Then, his loving, trusting wife, who insists she will "stand by his side," turns stool pigeon.

In one magazine article, she calls her husband a "flamboyant womanizer" and spares no details. He's a boozer, she tells the world.

The FBI wants to put the poor guy in shackles, and his wife is calling press conferences to tell about the holes in his underwear.

So John Jenrette decides to split for a few days. Who wouldn't want to get away from darling Rita at this point? And while he's gone, the roof really caves in.

He leaves her a bogus number in Miami, so she calls up reporters and announces she's filing for divorce. Then, she's packing her husband's clothes in their Washington townhouse and she comes across a shoe box filled with large bills that amount to $25,000.

Where do you think the money came from, Mrs. Jenrette?

"Probably my husband's take from Abscam," she answers. Whatever happened to "love, honor, and keep your trap shut while the heat's still on?"

Why didn't she say her husband follows little old ladies to the bank and then robs them of their Social Security payments to get all that money? She couldn't have made it any worse on the poor fellow.

Rita Jenrette has been on my bad side ever since she wagged her tongue at Moose Clubs and said she didn't want to go back to another one because the men all walk around with antlers on their heads.

What does Rita Jenrette know? Think of the good that Moose Clubs do simply by never turning away a thirsty wanderer traveling through an otherwise dry province.

I think Rita Jenrette is trying to attract attention to herself, and I wish she would go away. She is a very dangerous woman, as a matter of fact. What if all wives decided to blow the whistle on their husbands when they caught them in a little hanky-panky?

My wife could tell the world I don't pick up after myself, and that I snore, and that I am afraid to take shots, and that I won't watch horror movies alone, and that sometimes I forget to change socks for days, and that one of my little toes is bigger than the other one.

One of my little toes IS bigger than the other one. That is because one night I was walking through the house barefoot with no lights on and rammed one of my little toes into a sofa leg. And it still is swollen and roughly twice the size of my other little toe and it is shaped sort of like Idaho.

What I was doing walking through the house barefoot with no lights on is, I was headed to the kitchen for a cold pork chop.

There is something comforting about a cold pork chop. Unless, I would imagine, you're married to one like Rita Jenrette.

The Orange Sherbet Room

I promised myself that after I got married again, I wouldn't write those boring domestic sort of columns nobody really wants to read.

But the other day I came home from work and found my wife with two men who were doing something very strange in the living room of our new house.

They were painting the walls orange sherbet.

"What do you think?" asked my wife, beaming.

"You're doing our living room in early banana split?" I asked.

"You don't love me," said my wife.

I do love my wife, but I never have seen the walls of a living room painted the color of orange sherbet.

You know what orange sherbet looks like. Deer hunters wear vests that color so that other deer hunters can spot them in the underbrush a half-mile away and won't think they are deer and blow holes in them. Nobody will ever shoot a deer hunter in my living room.

Decorating a new house has been a completely unique experience for me. When I was a bachelor, which I have been on a number of occasions, it never took me very long to decorate my living quarters.

I had a black Naugahyde couch I always put in the living room, despite the fact that some liberal got up a drive to do away with Naugahyde couches because of the number of little Naugas they had to hit in the head with lead pipes to make even one Naugahyde ottoman.

I usually mounted a velvet portrait of a bullfighter somewhere, a picture of me shooting a basketball in the tenth grade, a Willie Nelson poster, and the plaque they gave me when I covered the Liberty Bowl football game in 1967 that says I am an honorary citizen of Memphis, even though I never have forgiven that city for not disappearing with the Mississippi riverboats.

Most apartments don't have dens, so I didn't have to worry about decorating my den.

If I had had a den, I probably would have put my collection of twenty-four beer bottles from all over the world there, and I also would have spread some *Playboy* and *Time* magazines around, to say that I not only was with it sexually and socially, but I also knew Hodding Carter was not the name of a new plant food.

My bedroom, you ask? Va-va-voom, my bedroom, they ask! Double mattress with a sag on one side and the Roy Rogers spread my mom bought me when I was ten.

Decorating our new house, I have learned I needed a lot of things I never knew I needed.

Ten zillion houseplants, for instance. *Plants?* In the hallways, my wife has planted a couple of *trees*. They're called *foyerus interruptus* or some such, and the kids want me to build them a house in the top of one.

We have new light fixtures, ceiling fans, French doors that separate this room from that room, more new bookshelves than your local public library, and lots of new trinkets.

I mean, we have *lots* of new trinkets. Little glass doodads that look sort of like the glass blower was on glue or something. In order to get ready for Christmas early, we even have a five-decked, glass-enclosed set of figurines that depict the first fifteen years of the life of Christ.

We have a wood-carved pig, four brass ducks, and fifteen paintings of flowers and little girls in bonnets. And nothing made out of Naugahyde.

"What effect," I asked my wife, "are you trying to create with a room the color of orange sherbet?"

"You have no taste whatsoever," she replied. "It's not orange sherbet, it's 'coral,' and I want an outside-indoors effect, Bahamian, sort of Humphrey Bogart in *Casablanca*, Rick's Bar with the ceiling fan and all of that."

I went down to the basement where all my old

furniture is stored, dusted off my black Nauga-hyde couch, and took a nap.

Tips for No. 3

When actor Ryan O'Neal gets married to actress Farrah Fawcett, Ryan O'Neal and I will have something in common. We both will be into our third marriage.

Mr. O'Neal and Miss Fawcett plan to tie the knot as soon as possible, the couple announced recently from Venice, which is something Mr. O'Neal and I don't have in common.

I made the announcement of my engagement to No. 3 while standing on the bar in a beer joint located just on the outskirts of Fort Deposit, Alabama.

You would be surprised how many people get married for the third time. A close friend of mine also just got married for the third time.

"Couple more of these," he said to me at the reception after the wedding, "and we'll have enough (ex's) between us for a girls' field hockey team with two cheerleaders."

I didn't think that was very funny, and neither did my friend's new bride, who elbowed him in the belly when he said it.

I wish Mr. O'Neal and Miss Fawcett the very best. They deserve each other, say Hollywood insiders.

I just hope Mr. O'Neal realizes it's different the third time around. The first time you have no earthly idea what you are getting into, and you normally botch it.

The second time, you are a veteran, but still prone to many rookie mistakes. If you go back a third time, you have entered the big leagues, and there can be no more excuses.

Around poker tables, they have a saying: "Put up or shut up, cowboy." The same applies to a man entering his third marriage.

I have nearly eight months of being married for the third time under my belt. It has been a learning experience, from which I now offer the following advice to Mr. O'Neal and to any other man about to go for a three-bagger, an awful choice of words.

How to make it work the third time around:

● Go shopping in antique stores with her once in a while, even if it absolutely kills you. It beats shopping for antiques in a bar at midnight, which, you must realize by now, is no fun at all.

● Don't complain if she puts a black sock with a navy blue sock. Life is too short to spend one second worrying about socks.

● Don't come home a-drinkin' with lovin' on your mind. (Loretta Lynn said that before I did, but it's still strong advice.)

● Don't fool around.

● If you are going to fool around anyway,

when you get caught (notice I said, "when" instead of "if"), lie like a dog.

● Speaking of lying, tell her she's pretty even when she isn't wearing make-up and her hair is in curlers and she's wearing flip-flops and your old football jersey.

● Don't give her a new blade for her hacksaw on your anniversary.

● Shop for her underwear.

● Pick yours up off the lousy bedroom floor once in a while.

● When you are in a restaurant alone with just her, the champagne, and the candlelight, never say, "You know, this place has really gone downhill since I and (a) my first wife, (b) my second wife, were here."

● Keep a bottle of mouthwash on your bedside table.

● Have some laughing children around.

● Refuse all telephone numbers.

● When there is obviously something wrong with her, and you ask, "What's wrong with you?" and she replies, "Nothing," leave the house immediately. There is something wrong with her.

● Forget candy and flowers. By now you must have figured out what they really like are airplane tickets to places where the sun shines, and Volvos.

● Her back itches, too, dummy. You scratch occasionally.

● Above all, being married the third time

means always having to say you're sorry. If you had done that the first two times instead of pouting, there wouldn't have been the need for a third time.

White Bread or Bust

My wife has insisted I give up white bread.

"There is absolutely no food value in white bread," she informed me.

"But it tastes good," I replied.

"Hedonist," said my wife.

I've given up so much already. I'm not supposed to eat a lot of eggs or drink a lot of milk because of cholesterol. Cake and pie and candy do something strange to my blood-sugar level.

Cokes. I used to drink a lot of Cokes, but the doctor said switch to diet drinks. On diet drink cans, there is a warning about saccharin causing cancer in laboratory animals. I assume those animals are rats.

I don't worry about rats getting cancer that much. Rats are little and they just sort of look unhealthy in the first place. When they find out a couple of Diet Pepsis will give an elephant cancer, I'll become much more concerned.

What else? I don't smoke anymore. I gave up vodka tonics out of respect for my head and liver. Now that I'm married again, I'm on the streets a lot less.

White bread was sort of my last holdout. Let me tell you what I like about white bread:

It's soft. I hate hard bread. When I lived in Chicago, all they ever served in restaurants was hard, dark bread.

"What will you have, sir?" the waitress would ask.

"Tuna salad, hold the hockey pucks," I would reply.

"Tuna salad, no bread!" the waitress would scream to the cook.

How I longed for some of those marvelous, delicious "brown 'n' serve" rolls, the kind they used to serve in truck stop restaurants of my youth with the $1.25 hamburger steak (which is now the "chopped sirloin" that goes for seven bucks).

White bread makes better sandwiches, too. Take, for example, a banana sandwich, a rare delicacy I used to carry to school for lunch. Cover the inside of two pieces of white bread with mayonnaise, then put the bread around several slices of barely ripe banana, and the result is divine.

Imagine a banana sandwich on dark, hard bread. The more thought of such a hideous concoction turns my stomach.

"Go ahead and eat white bread and ruin your digestive system and see if I care," my wife says.

"Toast me a loaf of that dark bread and I'll go replace the shingles on the roof," I reply, and the white bread/dark bread debate is off and running again.

She will win in the end, of course. I will give up white bread, just like I did all the other pleasures I miss.

But I have made one promise to myself that I hope I am allowed to keep. It is a dream that is constant:

On my sixty-fifth birthday, I am going to a nice, cool place like the grassy bank of a river. I am going to take with me a carton of Marlboro cigarettes, a quart of vodka, several bottles of tonic, lime, and crushed ice, a loaf of thinly sliced white bread, mayonnaise, a banana, and a nineteen-year-old girl.

I am going to smoke all the Marlboro cigarettes, drink all the vodka tonics I please, and top it all off with a banana sandwich on white.

The nineteen-year-old girl?

After I've finished with all the other stuff and if I'm still alive, I will sing her a love song.

"Love" Versus "Lust"

I always try to listen closely when the pope makes one of his official statements. As I understand it, His Holyship has one of the better pipelines to the Big Rulemaker, and I don't want to miss anything I might be tested on later.

But I, along with millions of others, was caught

completely off guard with the recent papal pronouncement that it is a sin to lust after your own wife.

Now there's a real kick in the libido if I ever heard one.

We went all through this lust business four years ago when soon-to-be-elected President Carter admitted he had "lusted in his heart" after women other than the voluptuous Rosalynn.

What is it about the presidential election? Four years later, soon-to-be-unelected President Carter hasn't got time to lust after anybody with Ronald Reagan on his back, but it's the pope, of all people, who brings the subject up again.

I like the pope. He's got a nice smile. He appears to have a sense of humor, and he is a warm, sensitive man of peace.

But he doesn't know beans when it comes to love and lust. Otherwise, he couldn't have become pope, if you know what I mean.

But a worldly person like myself, well, I know my share about love, and I have personally lusted on a number of occasions, most recently during the movie *Dressed to Kill*, starring Angie Dickinson.

A man who can watch Angie Dickinson in certain scenes in *Dressed to Kill* and think about needing more salt for his popcorn is badly in need of an oil change.

And as far as lusting after one's wife is concerned, that's been the problem for a long time now. Instead of lusting after their wives, men have been lusting after their secretaries and their neighbors' wives, and the 8.5 at the end of the bar. And if more men would, in fact, lust after what's in their own ballpark, watch the bottom fall out of the divorce rate.

I've read a number of explanations of "what the pope was trying to say." The best one said what the pope meant was a man should "love" his wife and not merely "lust" after her as a "sex object."

Okay, I think most men can certainly live within those boundaries.

But before we put this matter to bed, or rest, maybe we should make some clear distinctions between "love" and "lust."

"Love" is when you bring her home a present and it is not a special occasion.

"Lust" is when you bought it at Frederick's of Hollywood, and Candy Barr wouldn't be caught dead wearing it.

"Love" is when you take a romantic cruise together aboard a sailboat.

"Lust" is when the boat belongs to her husband, who is in Cleveland on business.

"Love" is when you met at a church social.

"Lust" is when she answered your ad in *Hustler*.

"Love" is when she watches "The NFL Today" to learn all of football's positions.

"Lust" is when you have memorized every diagram in *More of the Joy of Sex*.

"Love" is when he invites you to a movie.

"Lust" is when it is playing in his bedroom, the one with the mirrors and burning incense.

Got the picture? What a fun column to write, and I would like to point out just one more thing before I go:

Is it just my imagination that the people who usually are the most vocal about sex also are the people who engage in it the least?

Nineteen Was a Long Time Ago

She was ten the first time I saw her. So was I. She was tall and gangly and put together sort of funny.

"Is that girl going to be in our class?" asked one of my pals as we looked her over the first day of the new school year.

"I hope not," I said. The last thing we needed in the sixth grade, I reasoned, was another girl. What we needed was a good second baseman. Funny how childish priorities go.

But we both grew, she out of her gangliness. Suddenly her proportions were nearly perfect. Me, I was out of my preoccupation with baseball and into a keen interest in the opposite sex.

It was in the ninth grade that the whole blasted thing began. We went on a Sunday school hayride together, and I had never been kissed until I was kissed by her, and so, six years later, I married her.

You don't know a damn thing when you are nineteen. It should be against the law to get married when you are nineteen.

But I was spending every week missing her, and I was absolutely terrible and out of place with anybody else. I knew when I was thirteen that I would marry her, so why wait any longer?

The little church was packed. My best man, as we stood in the anteroom awaiting her arrival down the aisle, said to me:

"Look, stupid. I can have us both 500 miles away from here by morning. Just say the word."

The next morning I was in our honeymoon bed.

We lasted—I forget exactly—four years, maybe. What went wrong? I'll tell you what went wrong. We were kids, children.

I went one way in my head. She went another. It broke our mothers' hearts.

So there I am in this huge department store and people are running all around doing their Christmas shopping, and the last person I figured I would run into, I ran into.

She looked great. Still blonde and thin. Still with the fashion. We talked for fifteen minutes.

She lives in another city. She has a husband and two kids. She was home just for a visit.

"Tell me about your wife," she said.

I raved.

"And how is it with you?" I asked.

"He's great," she replied. "I would have never made it without him.

"You always wanted to be a writer," she went on. "Are you satisfied now?"

"What's satisfied?" I asked back. "The more you get, the more you want. It's human."

We went back and forth like that. In these situations, there is another sense that takes over. You *sense* what to say, and what not to say, and what to ask about, and what not to ask about.

And you *sense*—simultaneously—when it is time to end it. The present reality hovers.

"We were so young, weren't we?" she asked, adjusting her coat to leave.

"We didn't know a damn thing," I answered.

"I'm such a different person now. All that back then is like a dream. God, how did you put up with me? Remember the time I cried when it was my birthday and you went to a ball game? How stupid."

"That wasn't stupid. I shouldn't have gone to the ball game."

"Do you still complain about your socks not being matcd exactly right?"

"Yeah. My wife goes nuts when I do that."

"There is one good thing, though," she said.

"What's that?"

"Neither one of us got fat, did we?"

"No, neither one of us got fat."

I took her hand and shook it. She went one way. I went another.

7

CATS AND DOGS

The more I think about it, I really don't dislike cats. It's cat-lovers who are dangerous, and that is explained in detail here. As for dogs, I've never had one to ask, "Where have you been for so long?" "Why didn't you call if you knew you were going to be late?" and "Why do we never talk?" If for no other reason, I appreciate dogs for never having asked me questions I prefer not to answer. . . .

"Butterbean" Goes to Camp

I first thought our dog, who is large and shaggy, was mentally retarded. That is because our dog was doing some strange things. I will list some of the strange things our dog was doing.

● Eating plants. House plants, out-of-the-house plants, also trees and flowers. Imagine this big, shaggy dog walking up to a blooming hybeiwhatzit and eating the sucker, petal by petal. If there were any bugs or bees in the plants or flowers that fell victim to my dog, she would eat them too.

● Wrestling with our youngest child. He is four and about a third the size of our dog. Our dog was making the child's life miserable. Whenever the child made any sort of quick move, the dog would think he wanted to wrestle her, and she would pounce upon the poor little snipper and flip him around like he was no more than a stuffed toy. The child would cry, quite obviously, which would make the dog bark. None of this sort of thing ever happened to me when I was single.

● Running away from home. I spent a great deal of money on a fence for my dog. She would have been out of Alcatraz in eight seconds. My dog would dig her way under the fence and then disappear and I would have to go look for her. Once she escaped and I found her talking to sailors in a bar in Norfolk.

On top of all that, our dog was quite disobedient. "Butterbean" (not her real name) would not come when you called her, nor would she do any tricks, nor would she eat anywhere but seated at the table. (She would wrestle the four-year-old for his chair, then tease and tantalize him with scraps and bites from her plate, poor kid.)

As head of the family, I decided to do something about our dog. I took her to the vet.

"There is nothing wrong with your dog mentally," said my vet. "She's just a high-strung animal with a dominating personality. You should send her to obedience camp."

Dogs go to camp? Certainly, said my vet, and when they return they don't eat plants, terrorize four-year-olds or hustle drinks off sailors, and actually will eat Alpo off a dish on the back porch.

This I had to see, so I enrolled our dog in an obedience camp. The first week was murder. She short-sheeted two counselors, mugged poodles for their canteen money and called at two o'clock in the morning, collect, howling to come home.

At the end of the week I had to pay for the damages she had caused (she chewed up all the volleyballs and flushed cherry bombs down the commodes) and then pleaded with the camp director, who once trained killer dogs for combat, to allow her to stay.

"Dogs will be dogs," I laughed.

"Your mutt's a menace to society," he said.

The second week, things began to get a little better. She made a friend—a Doberman. They chased alligators together in a nearby swamp, then shared a large tree for lunch.

Counselors reported her to be less aggressive and even taking part in the crafts classes. She made a leather belt and a wallet with "Dad" etched across the front. I must say I was touched.

The third week, she wasn't the same dog at all. She was elected council representative from her kennel and even had begun helping some of the younger, less experienced campers learn the ropes.

"Dear Mr. Grizzard," the camp director wrote me after the third week. "I am happy to say 'Butterbean' (not her real name) is progressing wonderfully, and she will be able to come home very soon."

Well, that day finally has arrived. This afternoon I will drive out to the obedience camp to pick up our dog. Despite all the problems in the past, we've missed the old girl, and it will be nice to have her home.

The thing with the Doberman never worked out, incidentally. One afternoon he tried to get fresh with our dog and she broke three of his paws, tied a knot in his tail, and put him in the camp infirmary for six weeks.

The Comeback Cat

I have a very real problem at my house involving a cat. I don't like cats. I never have liked cats. I never will like cats, and that is the problem.

A cat has moved into my house. I went out of town for a couple of days. When I returned, I opened the front door, and there stood a cat—a brown cat with a speck of white on its tail.

I say "its" tail because I don't know if the cat is a boy or a girl, and I don't know how to tell the difference without resorting to some unthinkable snooping.

First, I asked the cat a question, which was an idiotic thing to do, but have you ever noticed how people are always asking their pets, especially cats, questions?

"Mommie's little darling want some din-din?" Etc.

I asked the cat, "How did you get inside my house?"

The doors had been locked. The windows

were secure. Maybe the cat came down the chimney?

"Did you come down the chimney?" I asked the cat.

I did it again. I asked a dumb animal a question. What do you do next, stupid, suggest a couple of games of backgammon?

I shooed the cat out of my house, and so much for my cat problem.

Hardly. The next morning, I awakened to something furry crawling around on my head. The cat was back, and the cat was in my bed. That's impossible. I had put the cat out myself, and I had locked the doors and pulled the damper down the chimney.

"Who put you up to this?" I asked the cat, obviously no longer in control of my faculties.

I put the cat out again.

But the cat came back. Don't ask me how the cat gets into my house, but it does. I finally reached such a point of frustration that I enlisted the help of one of my neighbors, Mrs. Framingham, a worrisome old biddy who keeps a lot of cats around. I told her how the cat was driving me up a wall.

"You wouldn't hurt the little darling, would you?" Mrs. Framingham asked me.

"I wouldn't consider any permanent injuries," I responded.

"You lay one hand on that cat, and I'll break both your arms," said Mrs. Framingham, who had a typical cat-lover's attitude: Be kind to animals, or I'll break your nose.

"Why not give the poor little creature a chance?" she went on. "It obviously likes you, and it needs a home. Why not just accept it?"

No way. Cats are sneaky—and try to get a cat to roll over and play dead or chase a stick or do all the neat things a dog will do.

Cats think they are above that. Plus, I don't want a pet that bathes more often than I do.

"Shush," said Mrs. Framingham. "Give the poor dear two weeks. In two weeks you will love it. The two of you will be inseparable. That's the beauty of cats. They grow on you."

I gave the cat two weeks. I still don't want a cat. Besides, while I was typing this, I thought of an obvious solution to the problem.

All I have to do is make the cat feel unwanted. No rough stuff, just a few subtle hints that no purring, meowing little pest is going to get the best of me, no matter what the old bat down the street says.

You don't think I mean it? From now on, daddy's little precious is going to have to sleep in its own room. And our trip to the basketball game next week is definitely off.

Scooter

Kathy Williams is an attorney. She lives in Avondale, a suburb of Atlanta. Until five months ago, she lived alone. Then, Scooter came to live with her.

Scooter was a fuzzy brown puppy. If he had any papers, he didn't have them on him.

"He just walked up out of nowhere," said Kathy Williams. "He was wearing a collar, but he had no license. I fed him. He just stayed. He would hang around in my back yard, except when he walked across the street to play with the children over there. He loved children. And they loved him."

One day she came home from work and Scooter was gone. Dogs often wander away. He would be back.

He never came back.

"What was so funny about this was I had never really cared about dogs before," Kathy Williams explained. "But there was something about this little dog. I called him 'Scooter' because he sort of scooted along on his tummy when he ran. He was just a mixed breed, but after he was gone, I really missed him."

For five weeks, Scooter was missing. Kathy Williams put an ad in the paper, under "Lost Dogs." She watched the papers to see if anybody might have found her dog.

There is a lake in Avondale. Every night she would walk around the lake and call for her dog, hoping he might return.

What else she did was visit DeKalb County

Animal Control once a week to see if Scooter had been picked up.

"I was so afraid they would find him and kill him before I could claim him," she said. "I told everybody down there what he looked like, and I had them on alert for my dog."

Last Tuesday, Kathy Williams made her weekly visit to the DeKalb pound. She found Scooter.

"I've never been so excited in my life," she said. "I couldn't wait to get him out of there."

Here is where the plot thickens.

A woman at the desk told Kathy Williams not to reclaim her dog. When a dog is picked up in DeKalb County, she explained, an officer writes out a citation for whomever reclaims the dog. That person then has to go to court and pay a fine for violating the DeKalb leash law.

"She told me to wait until Thursday, when Scooter had been in the pound for seven days, and then I could just adopt him. That would cost me $41, but he got shots and everything, and I wouldn't have to go to court or pay a fine," Kathy Williams explained.

"I walked back into the cage area, and there was this guy named Jeff, and he told me to do the same thing. I mentioned I really didn't own the dog, that he had just taken up at my house, but he said it didn't matter. If I reclaimed the dog, then I would have to get the ticket."

Kathy Williams took the advice. Before she left, however, she made certain everybody involved knew to make certain nothing happened to Scooter.

"They laughed at me because I went on about it for so long," she said. "But I just couldn't have anything happen to my dog."

Kathy Williams left Scooter at the pound. Thursday morning, she returned to pick him up. On her way, she stopped to buy him a new collar, some flea and tick powder, and a Slim-Jim as a reward.

"When I walked into the place, I could sense something was wrong," she said. "I went back to the cage where Scooter had been, and he wasn't in there." Kathy Williams started asking about her dog. Nobody would give her a straight answer. Finally, somebody gave her a straight answer. There had been a mistake. Scooter had been killed.

"They tried to give me another dog," said Kathy Williams. "I didn't want another dog. I wanted Scooter."

"We made a terrible mistake," said Major Harold Davis, who is in charge of the DeKalb facility. "A note was written and attached to a dog, saying to hold the dog for the lady. But the note was placed on the wrong dog.

"But people ought to think about these things. If your dog gets picked up, don't take a chance. Get that rascal out of here. Take the ticket. Pay the fine."

Kathy Williams isn't sleeping so well these nights because she didn't do exactly that. But why was she given advice to the contrary by personnel at the pound?

And how could somebody be careless enough to kill the wrong dog?

"I told that lady," said Major Davis, "when she gets ready for another pet, to call us. We'll help her in any way we can."

A nice gesture. But somehow I get the feeling she won't be calling.

Pet Killer

You have to know basset hounds to love them. I have known and loved two. I lost one in a custody battle. The other, who is three months old, lives in my house now. The dog's name is Barney. Soon he will be the size, and shape, of a canoe.

Somebody else who owns a basset hound was telling me, "They're awful dogs, really. They bark too much, they get their ears in their food and then they get their ears on everything in the house, they won't mind, and they shed all over your furniture.

"But you take one look at those big, sad eyes and you're hooked."

I know the feeling. So do Tom and Diana Thorington of Atlanta. They have a basset hound. His name is Lance. He's two years old and he has national champions on both sides of his family. (If you really love a dog, it doesn't matter if his pedigree is more impressive than your own.)

A couple of weeks ago the Thoringtons took Lance when they went to an afternoon party at a friend's house. The friend has a large lot, so they let Lance out to play with the friend's dog, a mutt. Basset hounds are not snooty.

Sometime later the people at the party heard shots being fired across the way at a neighbor's house. The host of the party and the neighbor were not close friends. Soon you will see why.

The host and Tom Thorington left the party to see what the shooting was about. They saw the neighbor firing away at Lance and the mutt.

When they reached the man, the mutt was already dead. They didn't see Lance.

"Did you shoot my dog?" Tom Thorington screamed at the man.

"Shot two of 'em," the man replied, laughing.

"You are a rotten, no-good son of a bitch," said Tom Thorington, who was being nice.

The man put his rifle, a .22, to Tom Thorington's chest.

"I think I'll shoot you next," he said.

Tom and his friend started to walk away.

"I'll shoot you in the back," said the man.

Tom and his friend kept walking. They got lucky. Crazy with the rifle didn't shoot.

Tom began calling to Lance. A couple of minutes later he heard a muffled sound from the weeds. It was Lance, with four bullets in his throat. And more, all over his body. There were even bullet holes in Lance's long, floppy ears.

"He was shot at least *ten* times," Diana Thorington told me later. "Can you imagine somebody sighting down on a basset hound TEN times?"

I've never heard of a blacker heart.

The Thoringtons rushed Lance to the local vet.

"The vet told us to forget it," said Diana. "He said there was no way Lance would make it. But we begged him to try. We love that dog so much."

Another dog, named Rip, gave some blood, and a miracle happened. Lance lived.

Okay, some nut shoots your dog and then threatens to shoot you. What do you do about it?

"We went to the police," said Diana Thorington, "but they said there was nothing much they could do. The laws about shooting dogs are pretty weak. The police said if we filed charges it would just mean a big hassle, and probably nothing much would come of it. The man was on his own property."

It is not written that life must necessarily be fair. So the Thoringtons' friend's dog is dead, and the Thoringtons' basset hound, with a little help from his friend, barely made it, and el sicko with the gun is still off his leash.

It *is* written, however, that a creep who would kill one family pet and then pull a trigger ten times on what is one of God's most loving creatures will, sooner or later, get his.

Every dog has his day, so to speak. Knowing that, I rest a little easier. Not much, but a little.

8

SPECIAL OCCASIONS

The holidays. They bring out the best and the worst in people. April 15 is not a holiday, of course, but it should be. It brings out the most in people ....

The Morning After

News item: Another New Year's Eve is just around the corner.

"Harvey, wake up, Harvey."

"Whatsmattah?"

"Nothing's the matter, Harvey. I just want you to wake up."

"Whatimeisit?"

"Past 10, Harvey."

"Gladys, why do I have to wake up, Gladys? It's New Year's Day. I wanna sleep until the football games."

"I can't sleep, Harvey. Not after your performance last night."

"What did I do last night?"

"You don't remember?"

"I don't remember, Gladys. I was drunk."

"Drunk? 'Drunk' isn't the word for it, Harvey

167

You were 'blitzed.' You were 'stoned.' You were sickening."

"What could I have possibly done that was so bad, Gladys?"

"I'll tell you what you did. You made an absolute fool out of yourself at the Blantons' party. I can never show my face in this neighborhood again."

"So I got a little drunk. It was New Year's Eve, Gladys. I always get drunk on New Year's Eve."

"Harvey, you danced with Harriet Blanton's dog all night long."

"So?"

"So you thought you were dancing with Harriet Blanton. You told the dog how much you were enjoying the hors d'oeuvres and you tried to get Harriet to roll over for a sausage ball."

"I did that?"

"That's not all, Harvey."

"Omigod. What else?"

"You got into a fight with Ralph Beetleman."

"The skinny guy with the fat wife?"

"Gloria."

"Gloria who?"

"Gloria Beetleman, Ralph Beetleman's wife. She's the reason for the fight. You asked Ralph what he fed his land whale."

"I said that?"

"You said it, Harvey. Then, Ralph Beetleman took a punch at you. He missed, but Gloria kneed you in the belly and you were out for half an hour."

"So I danced with a dog and insulted a beer truck. Big deal, Gladys."

"There's more, Harvey. You poured a drink on Mildred Pillingham."

"Where?"

"In the living room."

"No, I mean...."

"Down the front of her dress, Harvey. Mildred Pillingham is in my car pool."

"I don't want to hear any more, Gladys."

"You're going to hear it, Harvey. I am ruined in this town, and you are going to hear it all. You burned a hole in the Blantons' new couch with a cigarette. You ate the floral arrangement in the dining room. You put your head in the punch bowl, and when the party was over, we found you in the backyard howling at the moon."

"With Harriet Blanton's dog?"

"With Harriet Blanton. She got just as wasted as you did."

Artie's Tax Service

Some people, believe it or not, actually file their income tax returns weeks and months ahead of the dreaded April 15 deadline. These people are normally well off, and they have their own accountants and use their refund checks to go to resorts in Mexico or the Caribbean.

(You may be asking, "What is a refund check?" Don't bother. It would only confuse you.)

I feel sorry for these people. They don't realize what fun and excitement they are missing by not waiting until the last minute to have their income taxes prepared.

It is the same thrill you get from waiting until the last minute to do your Christmas shopping or to rent a tuxedo for the annual Moose Lodge Dance and Fish Fry.

Procrastinators, like myself, enjoy the adventure and danger of living on the brink of disaster. Only a few days remain before the fifteenth, but I haven't even bothered to look for my W-2 forms yet.

That's because I can do what I always do— wait until a couple of hours before the deadline and pay a visit to Artie (Three Fingers) McGuirk's Friendly Tax Service and Pool and Recreation Hall.

You would love Artie's place. Get your taxes done, shoot a little pool or maybe talk to Artie about important sports questions like point spreads.

This is a special year at Artie's incidentally. Artie is back after a brief absence. Ask where Artie has been, and one of his friendly goons, er, associates, will answer simply, "On a long trip. What's it to ya?"

Of course, there are other places I could go

to get my taxes done at the eleventh hour. You hear about them on television about this time every year.

There is Mr. Loophole Tax Service, for instance. What bothers me about Mr. Loophole, however, is all the offices are in trailers sitting in shopping center parking lots. What if I am audited and come back to Mr. Loophole looking for help and there is a shopping center carnival where the trailer used to be parked?

Then, there's H&R Schlock. The man in the three-piece suit, seated in a comfortable chair, comes on the screen and tells you all the reasons you should use his tax service.

"Reason No. 11 for using H&R Schlock Tax Service: If the IRS calls you in for an audit, we'll give you a new tie for your appointment."

Artie and his trained staff of professionals offer even more:

● All preparations and consultations are strictly confidential. As Artie says, "One peep about who fixed this return, and you'll sleep with the fishes."

● All possible deductions are taken. Artie is very careful here. One year he missed some deductions for one of his best clients, Crazy Carlo (The Shark) DeRogatis, and Crazy Carlo deducted two of Artie's fingers as a penalty.

● Each member of Artie's staff has spent years learning about taxes. One spent ten to twenty in Joliet learning you can't hide the fifty Gs you picked up in a land fraud deal.

● If you are indicted and thrown into the slammer, Artie will send you cigarettes and reading material once a month until your release.

● If you do happen to get a refund check, Artie insists you bring it to him to be cashed. You pay only a small service charge of ninety-five percent.

● If you try to cash your refund check elsewhere and take a little trip to Mexico or the Caribbean, Artie will have a member of his staff consult with you further when you return—and your tax problems will be over.

Permanently.

Mayhem and Marshmallow Chickens

Millions of Americans will take part in the annual ritual of the Easter egg hunt today. The adults will hide candy eggs and other sugary surprises, and the children, dressed in their Easter finery, will vie to see who can fill his or her basket first.

Among other bad things that will happen, there will be a lot of arguments.

Larry, eight, and Debbi, five, will happen upon the chocolate bunny prize, hidden in the tall weeds near the swing set, at precisely the same moment.

"It's mine!" Larry will scream.

"I saw it first!" Debbi will counter.

Both children will begin to cry and pull at the chocolate bunny.

"Now, children," Larry's mom will interrupt. "Let's settle this fairly. Which of you is the oldest?"

"I am, Mom," Larry will say.

"Then you get the chocolate bunny prize," his mother will conclude. Mothers always take care of their own at an Easter egg hunt.

"Waaaaaaaa!" Debbi will scream, running to her mother. "Larry's mother took my chocolate bunny prize and gave it to Larry because he is older than me!"

"Don't worry, darling," Debbi's mom will say. "I'll fix that pushy broad."

A lot of hair-pulling and scratching and screaming later, the two adults will be pulled apart by the cops. Meanwhile, Larry has dropped the chocolate bunny prize onto the ground and the dog is eating it, and Debbi has brained a four-year-old for his marshmallow chicken.

That's another thing about Easter egg hunts. The younger the child, the more hazardous egg hunts can be to both the kid's mental and physical well-being.

Let's say you are two. You barely know how to locate your mouth. And they expect you to be able to run around in an open field and find Easter eggs?

The older kids will find eggs, of course. They'll find 'em by the dozens, but you won't have a blasted thing in your stupid basket, so you will get frustrated and you will start to cry because you feel inadequate. Later, when you flunk out of college and join a religious cult, it will all be because you couldn't find an egg when you were two.

There also is the chance you won't live through the egg hunt in order to grow up to be a total failure. Kids are vicious when it comes to eggs. They will trample other children, hit other children with sticks, kick other children—whatever it takes to wrest an egg from the possession of an opponent in the hunt.

We used to have egg hunts at my school. I hated them because of Frankie Garfield, the school bully. At first, Frankie would go to the trouble of actually making an effort to find his own eggs.

But bending over to pick up eggs was a lot of work for Frankie, so he eventually took to waiting until after school and then searching through every kid's basket and taking his pick of the loot.

Once he caught Alvin Bates hiding a creme-filled duck in his back pocket. Frankie decorated Alvin's face with the creme-filled duck and then hit him in the belly. Alvin always stayed home sick after that on egg hunt day.

The cruelest Easter egg hunt story I know, however, occurred in Philadelphia, where they put on an egg hunt for children in the outfield grass before a Phillies baseball game. The fans booed the kids who couldn't find eggs.

There is something about an Easter egg hunt that brings out the worst in all of us.

A Mother's Side of the Story

Lillian Pye had a son. His name was James Scroggins, and he was an Atlanta policeman, like his daddy before him. He was also a husband and the father of three children.

James Scroggins was thirty when he died last October. Lillian Pye remembers every detail of what happened to her son.

"He had worked his regular day shift at the police department," she began as we talked last week. As we talked, I could hear the hurt in her voice. It still runs deep.

"He went home, and then he got in his car, a Volkswagen, and started for night classes at DeKalb South. He wasn't drinking or anything. He was just going to class.

"There was this other car, and an eighteen-year-old was driving it. A boy. He lost control of his car. He hit a bridge, and then he ran into my son. The boy's car skidded 500 feet.

"It took them two and one half hours to cut my son out of the car. They would never even let me see the car. All he ever said after the

175

wreck was, 'I'm an Atlanta policeman. Take me to Grady.' He knew Grady had the best when it came to emergencies."

When they finally got Lillian Pye's son out of his car, it was too late to do anything more for him.

The other driver wasn't seriously injured. It happens that way sometimes.

"He was drunk," Lillian Pye said. "That boy was drunk." There is bitterness to go with her hurt.

"They told me when they took him out of the car, he was filthy and nasty and he was drunk."

DeKalb County charged the other driver with vehicular homicide. He went to trial. I'll let Lillian Pye tell the rest of it.

"At the trial, you should have seen that boy. His lawyer had told him exactly what to do. He had gotten a shave and a close haircut. He had on a new suit of clothes. He pleaded for mercy from the court.

"And you know what the judge gave him? He gave the boy five years probation and a $1,000 fine. That's it. Five years probation and a $1,000 fine. My son was killed, and that boy got off free. They didn't even take his license away.

"And you know something else? We never heard from him, and we never heard from his family. Not one word. They didn't even want to know if my son's wife and children could keep a roof over their heads, and they had a rough time of it until all the insurance was settled.

"I wrote the judge a letter and I said, 'I know you have a job to do, but you didn't do it very well.' I don't want that boy to get away with this. I don't want him driving around so he can do the same thing again."

I talked to DeKalb traffic investigators about the accident that killed James Scroggins. They agree with Lillian Pye that justice wasn't done.

But there is nothing they can do now. There is nothing anybody can do.

On second thought, yes there is. Lillian Pye admits she's called "everybody in town," television commentators, newspaper people.

All she wanted, I think, was the opportunity to tell her side of the story.

Now, she's had that opportunity, and what we can do for her is listen.

A mother misses her dead son on Mother's Day. What we can do for her is listen and, if just for a moment, share her hurt and her frustration.

It's the least, the very least, we can do.

The Last Hunt

Thanksgiving reminds different people of different things. It always reminds me of the first and last time I went hunting. That is because the first and last time I went hunting was on Thanksgiving Day when I was twelve.

Going hunting after the big Thanksgiving

feast was sort of a tradition among the menfolk in my family, and when you were a boy child and reached the age of twelve, you finally were able to go along.

Imagine my glee when my grandfather and uncles and cousins explained what we would be doing on the annual Thanksgiving Day hunt:

First, we would carry these heavy guns and hike over half the county, through briars and under barbed-wire fences and down in gullies if that was where the dogs took us.

Then, if anybody happened to spot a rabbit, he would promptly blow it to bits.

After the Thanksgiving Day feast the year I was twelve, I hid in the pump house and hoped they would leave on the hunt without me.

"What's the matter, son?" asked my uncle when the dogs flushed me out. "You don't want to go hunting with the rest of the men?" He put a lot of emphasis on the "men."

I'd rather spend the afternoon with my foot caught under Grandma's rocking chair is what I wanted to say, but I didn't say that at all.

"I was just in here checking the pump," is what I did say, and then it was off to the woods on the hunt.

Let me tell you what I think about going hunting:

If you want to take a gun and go out and shoot down defenseless animals in the forest, that's your business.

I just happen to think hunting is unfair.

Maybe if they changed the rules of hunting, I would feel better about it.

What I would do is issue guns to all the deer and rabbits and ducks and whatever else people hunt.

If you think hunting is an exciting sport now, wait until your prey can shoot back.

I don't like to hunt, but I do like to fish. "Same thing as hunting," you might be saying.

Not at all. First, there are no guns involved in fishing. Second, the fish has a choice of whether or not to bite the hook.

Hunters will also argue that they go out in the woods and kill for food. I don't believe that, not with a Del Taco on practically every corner in town.

Anyway, back to my first and last hunting trip on Thanksgiving Day when I was twelve:

It was cold and wet, and we must have walked thirty miles.

"Your best bet to kill a rabbit," explained my uncle, "is to find one sitting on its bed. That way, you don't have to shoot a moving target."

I prayed not to find a rabbit sitting on its bed, or on anybody else's bed.

My prayer was answered. As a matter of fact, nobody in the group even fired a shot, and there was a lot of cursing the dratted luck at the end of the day. I think the dogs had a good time, but it doesn't take much to make a dog happy.

When it came time to go hunting the next

Thanksgiving, I feigned a strange seizure at the top of my voice, so nobody wanted to take me on the hunt because I would scare off the rabbits. Every year, I managed a new excuse. When I was eighteen I left home, and the question of going hunting has never come up.in my life since.

In summary, what I think about hunting may be likened unto the perspective on the matter of one Ralph "High-Lift" Turnipseed, a man in my hometown who walked funny—he lifted one leg much higher than the other when he walked because of something strong he once drank because the local bootlegger was on vacation.

"Goin' rabbit-huntin' today, High-Lift?" somebody asked him on the street one day.

"Hell, no," High-Lift responded. "I ain't lost no rabbits."

Double-Dose of Hard Times

The response to this plea for help for Betty Hubbard was incredible. She and her son got their kitchen table and much more. There is bad in the world and, sometimes, it seems to scream out to be noticed. But there is much good, too, and Christmas brings it forth in gushes.

Betty Hubbard sat on what was a piece of lawn furniture before somebody bent the frame.

Betty's son, Joey, who is fifteen, sat on the floor. I took one of Betty's two chairs. A second visitor sat in the other chair.

Betty Hubbard talked about her life. I caught myself looking away to avoid her eyes when she cried.

"I never thought I would come to anything like this," she said. "We ain't got a thing."

She is fifty. She looks older. She's been a "widow woman" for ten years. She has an older son who she says is a "bad influence" on young Joey.

She moved to Atlanta from neighboring Rockdale County to look for a fresh start for her and the boy.

She has asthma. She is unemployed. She and Joey live in a hole of an apartment near Grant Park.

"I apologize for the way this place looks," Betty said. "Me and Joey got out a bucket of water and scrubbed these floors, but it didn't do no good."

We are seated in the living room. There is a small table near the door. On the table are pictures of Betty's sons. Between the two chairs is a locker. There is a small lamp on the locker. It is the only light in the house.

There is no table in the kitchen. There are two bedrooms in the apartment, but only one bed.

"Joey has to sleep with me," said Betty Hubbard. "A lot of folks might have something to say about that, but if he don't sleep with me, then he has to sleep on the floor. I ain't lettin' my baby sleep on no floor. He's all I got."

The sky is gray, the weather is cold. For the first two weeks Betty and Joey were in the apartment, they did not have the money to have the gas and power turned on. They huddled under blankets and burned candles.

Betty gets $400 a month in welfare payments. She hands over $220 for the apartment. She's being robbed. She borrowed from her landlord to put down the deposits for the gas and power.

"We had a home once," Betty goes on, breaking into tears, "but it got away from me. It's hard for a widow woman and two boys."

There was a silence in the room.

"I don't lie to my doctor, so I won't lie to you," Betty Hubbard continued. "We've all done some drinking. Me, and both the boys. All it done was cause fighting and misunderstanding. But there were times we didn't have nothing to eat. Where there ain't nothing to eat and somebody comes around with a drink, you just can't help but take it."

Betty Hubbard's apartment is a curse. Crumpled magazines and newspapers on the floor. Towels over the windows. Something caught my eye hanging on the wall, a baby's Christmas stocking marked "Joey," and a Christmas scene torn from a calendar. Christmas finds the darndest places.

Hard times come in different degrees. Betty and her boy Joey have caught a double-dose.

They're flat busted and it's Christmas Eve. They don't ask much:

- Some pants for Joey. He has only one pair. He is thirty in the waist and thirty length.
- Some shoes for Betty. Her only pair are worn moccasins.
- A small bed for Joey. And something where the two of them could sit down for a meal.
- Food. They ate sardines and soda crackers for Thanksgiving.
- An old television. "A boy naturally wants a television," said Betty Hubbard. "When I get back on my feet, that's the first thing I'm going to do, get my boy a television."
- Employment. Betty, with her asthma, is limited. She says she is good with children and once worked in a nursery. Joey is strong.

You hear these stories every Christmas. And you can't help everybody. And there are probably people even more deserving than Betty and Joey Hubbard, and, besides, we've got our own families to take care of.

But when the party is over and the wrappings are off the gifts, and Friday brings back reality, Betty and Joey still won't have a kitchen table.

Christmas Moose Smooch

I was driving along and listening to Christmas carols on the radio, and I started thinking back to those wonderful days when I was a kid and we used to draw names for the annual class Christmas party.

What a blast that was. What fun to share Christmas gifts with your classmates.

A bunch of cheap, ungrateful toads, all of them.

In the third grade Alvin Bates got my name. Alvin Bates was the kind of kid who would bring a candy bar for afternoon recess and then lick it all over before taking a bite so nobody would ask him to share it.

In the third grade Alvin Bates gave me one of those stupid wooden paddles with the balls and the rubber strings attached. You hit the stupid ball with the stupid paddle and the stupid ball, attached to the rubber string, comes back and you hit it again.

Teriffic. Fun for any awkward child under six. For fifty-nine cents, which is exactly what Alvin Bates shelled out for the paddle and the ball, he could have bought me something useful and educational, like a copy of *Stag* magazine they kept on the back shelf at the drugstore.

Stag was nothing compared to the magazines they have today, but in 1954, seeing a picture of a lady in a girdle could make your month.

Later I reaped revenge. I drew Alvin's name in the fourth grade, and I gave him a subscription to *Boy's Life*. Anybody caught reading *Boy's Life* was obviously a complete (a) mama's boy, (b) nurd, (c) sissy, (d) wimp, (e) fruit, (f) several other things I can't mention here.

"Hey, Four-Eyes," we used to taunt Alvin on the playground, "what's the centerfold this month in *Boy's Life?* Picture of a pup tent?"

Alvin spent most of his fourth-grade year crying.

In the fifth grade, Frankie Garfield, the school bully, drew my name.

Having your name drawn by Frankie Garfield was both bad and good. The bad part was Frankie's usual gift wouldn't exactly fit under the class tree.

The good part was Frankie's gift was a promise he wouldn't beat you up for at least a week.

"I let you live, Duck-Face," Frankie would say.

The worst thing that ever happened to me, though, was in the sixth grade when Cordie Mae Poovey, the ugliest and meanest girl in school, drew my name.

Cordie Mae was from a poor family, and she never had much money to spend on a gift. A pair of socks, I figured. Or a box of peanut brittle.

Worse. I opened my gift from Cordie Mae, and all I found was an envelope with a note inside that read, "Merry Christmas. I give you the gift of love. One (1) kiss and one (1) hug. Meet me after school. Cordie Mae."

I'd kiss a pig first. And Cordie Mae was as strong as she smelled. She could break a couple of ribs.

After school I ran as fast as I could, but she finally chased me down, hammerlocked me, and then planted one right on my mouth. Smmmmmmmack!

"How'd you like that, big boy?" asked Cordie Mae.

"Ever smooched with a moose?" I answered.

"Ever been run over by a herd of reindeer?" replied Cordie Mae, who had no sense of humor whatsoever.

The swelling in my nose went down in a couple of days, but it was a week before my eyes opened again.

9

ELECTION YEAR

I covered the 1980 presidential election from New Hampshire in January to the Republican Convention in Detroit in July to the Democratic Convention in New York in August, and I was standing there with the rain falling on Plains when Jimmy Carter came home on Inauguration Day, beaten and tired. I am convinced anybody crazy enough to go through what a person has to go through to get elected president is very likely about halfway to being completely bananas by the time he spends the first night in the White House....

Too Late for the Duke

The more I think about it, the less I can find wrong with the fact that a movie star is running for president of the United States.

Look who else has run for that position in the past—surveyors, architects, several generals, a couple of newspaper editors, a bankrupt haberdasher, even a peanut farmer, lest we forget.

But did it have to be THAT movie actor? When this country finally got around to picking somebody off the silver screen to make the mad dash for the White House, did it have to be, as he has been described, "the Errol Flynn of the B-movies?"

Ronald Reagan, for crying out loud? *Love Is On The Air* Ronald Reagan? *That Hagen Girl* (with Shirley Temple) Ronald Reagan? Supporting actor to a chimpanzee in *Bedtime for Bonzo* Ronald Reagan?

Do you realize Ronald Reagan originally was cast for the lead in *Casablanca*? Can you imagine that? Reagan in the role Bogie made a classic?

Let's face it. Ronald Reagan may have been lousy in *Hellcats of the Navy*, but he was terrible in another clunker, as Grover Cleveland Alexander, the baseball player.

Of all the actors we had to choose from to run for president, we took the man who once sold 20-Mule Team Borax on "Death Valley Days"?

You're looking for a movie-actor president? Just consider who else was available that we passed up:

● HENRY FONDA: Looks like a president, talks like a president, acts like a president. Did anybody see Henry Fonda in *Fail Safe?* He played the president and wound up ordering the bomb dropped on New York City. I told you he would have made us a good president.

● JIMMY STEWART: Well, ah, it might, ah, take him a long, ah, time, to make, ah, a state of the, ah, union address, but at least, ah, everybody in the, ah, country could do, ah, an impression of the, ah, president, don't you, ah, see?

● WALTER PIDGEON: Tall, distinguished. Plays a lot of senators and other big shots. My mother always thought a lot of Walter Pidgeon.

● CHARLTON HESTON: Normally thought of as an airline pilot or a chariot racer, but be honest with yourself.

You want somebody in the Oval Office who can handle a crisis, right? So would you pick squatty Ronald Reagan with that funky hairdo of his, or tall, handsome Charlton Heston, last seen, incidentally, drowning heroically in a sewer following an earthquake?

● GREGORY PECK: I always have been a big Gregory Peck fan since I saw him in *The Man in the Gray Flannel Suit* and later in *To Kill A Mockingbird.*

Gregory Peck would not waffle on the issues. We elected Eisenhower, didn't we? Then give MacArthur his chance.

● ROBERT STACK: Law and order candidate. Congress starts acting up and Ness and the boys come around to straighten them out.

● CHARLES BRONSON: Want somebody to get tough with the Russians? Here is somebody to get tough with the Russians. "One more word out of you, Leonid, and I'll bust your face in." That kind of get-tough-with-the Russians.

But what am I saying here? Fonda, Stewart, Heston, etc. Lightweights, all of them, when you consider the man who should be in Ronald Reagan's shoes right now.

Tall in the saddle, he was. A soldier. Tough, but fair. A patriot. What this country needs is a good dose of true grit. He had it.

Ronald Reagan, Ronald Smeagan. This country decides it wants to elevate a movie actor to the threshold of the White House and we pussyfoot around until the Duke is unavailable.

Sort of makes you sick to your stomach, doesn't it, pilgrim?

"What He Meant to Say Was..."

To follow the presidential campaign, one can all but ignore the statements and charges of the candidates and other influential individuals and wait for the clarifications that always follow from aides.

Some notable examples to clip and save:

• Ronald Reagan implies President Carter supports the Ku Klux Klan by making a snide remark about the president opening his campaign in Tuscumbia, Alabama, which, according to Mr. Reagan, is "the birthplace of the Klan."

WHAT AIDES SAID MR. REAGAN REAL-LY MEANT TO SAY: "Governor Reagan really meant to say he wishes Coach Bear Bryant and the University of Alabama football team another great season.

"He would also like to add he wants to visit Tuscumbia, himself, very soon to see his dearest and oldest friend, Helen Keller, who he remembers so well as such a talented dancer in all those old Hollywood musicals."

• President Carter implies that Mr. Reagan is a racist.

WHAT AIDES SAID MR. CARTER REAL-LY MEANT TO SAY: "The President really meant to say Mr. Reagan is spending too much time 'racing' round the country making unwarranted attacks on his record. Also he wanted to mention that Mr. Reagan has solicited the campaign help of stock car 'racing' king Richard Petty.

"And just because the President's statements were misinterpreted while he was standing in the late Dr. Martin Luther King, Jr., hometown church, surrounded by every black leader from here to Satchel Paige, it must be considered only a mere coincidence."

● Mr. Reagan says the United States' efforts in the Vietnam War were for a "noble cause."

WHAT AIDES SAID MR. REAGAN REALLY MEANT TO SAY: "'Spanish-American' instead of 'Vietnam.' Just a mere slip of the tongue. It could happen to anybody."

● Mr. Reagan gets his Chinas mixed up.

HOW AIDES EXPLAINED THAT: "The governor didn't have his hand pocket world Atlas with him at the time, and even if he did, 'little' China appears as such a tiny speck, anybody could overlook it, like Rhode Island in our own country.

"Incidentally, the governor will be campaigning in that great state soon, and we hope everybody who can will be out to greet him when his plane lands at the airport in Hartford."

● President Carter charges that Mr. Reagan, if elected, would lead the country into war.

WHAT AIDES SAID MR. CARTER REALLY MEANT TO SAY: "What he really meant to say was if this nation ever has to go to war, then Mr. Reagan would be a terrific person to lead us into it. As a second lieutenant, for instance, up ahead of all the troops, trying to knock out an enemy machine gun nest."

● *Time Magazine* quotes Miss Lillian Carter as saying, "Sometimes when I take a look at my children, I wish I had remained a virgin."

WHAT MISS LILLIAN'S FRIENDS IN PLAINS SAID SHE REALLY MEANT TO SAY: "She really meant to say that sometimes when she takes a look at her children, she wishes she had remained a virgin."

● Dr. Bailey Smith, president of the Southern Baptist Convention, makes the statement that "God almighty does not hear the prayers of a Jew."

WHAT THE DEACONS SAID DR. SMITH REALLY MEANT TO SAY: "He really meant to say God doesn't listen to the prayers of Jews, or of hardly anybody else, on WEDNESDAYS. That's the day he takes off to listen to blow-hard politicians ask forgiveness for all the lies they've told the previous week."

Debates and Rat-Killings

The headline in Wednesday's paper said it all about Tuesday night's debate between Jimmy Carter and Ronald Reagan:

"Carter, Reagan Both Feel Goals Achieved in Debate."

Of course Carter and Reagan both felt their goals were achieved in the debate. That's the problem with presidential debates. They are not like wrestling matches where one guy runs another guy's head into one of the ring posts and you can pick a clear winner.

A presidential debate is more like a rat-killing.

I don't know how many of you have ever been to a big league rat-killing before, but they work like this:

The rat-killers, armed with .22 rifles, hide behind some bales of hay in the barn. Some corn has been spread about to entice the rats to enter the arena. The lights are turned out.

As soon as it sounds like there are a number of rats gnawing on the corn, the lights are turned on and the rats are momentarily blinded. The rat-killers then cut down on the rats from behind the hay bales with their .22s.

This sounds a little one-sided in favor of the rat-killers, and it is, but the rats do get a nice meal before being blown away, and because rats are such pests, they don't deserve a fair shake anyway.

And after the rat-killing is over, both sides can always rationalize a victory.

Let's say some of the rats get away:

"A clear victory for our side," says the spokesrat. "Those clowns couldn't hit a bull in the bohunkus with a bass fiddle."

"Another win for us," counters the head rat-killer. "We didn't want to shoot them all so we could have another rat-killing."

Rat-killings and presidential debates. Just alike. Also, throw arguments with your wife into the same category.

I did the only sane thing for the debate Tuesday night. I watched it in a bar. After the debate was over, I polled the joint.

Three drunks were for Carter. Three drunks were for Reagan. The bartender was a Libertarian, and the waitress likes Anderson because he reminds her of her uncle in Tupelo who has the local pocket-fisherman franchise.

I kept my own scorecard. I tried to be as fair as possible. Here is how I rated each man's performance:

● HAIR—Carter's was neatly parted on the side-of-the-week and appeared to have been blow-dried. Reagan, meanwhile, had apparently slicked it down with Royal Crown. Wetheadsville with enough Grecian Formula Nine to turn chalk black. HAIR TO CARTER.

● SMILE—Carter, for a smiler, didn't smile much. Perhaps he was having another flare-up of what George Brett had. Reagan smiles like used car dealers smile. SMILE TO REAGAN.

● SUIT—Robert Hall Ronnie looked like he just stepped off the cover of *GQ*. Unfortunately, a 1953 issue. SUIT TO CARTER.

● FACIAL COLOR—Carter looked like he

had just seen Lester Maddox seated on the panel of inquisitors. Reagan had been pancaked a golden brown. FACIAL COLOR TO REAGAN.

● GRASP OF THE FACTS—Neither candidate appeared to know as much as Barbara Walters. GRASP OF FACTS TO BARBARA WALTERS.

What I am going to do is declare the 1980 Great Presidential Debate a deadlock and make only one other observation:

I wouldn't take Barbara Walters to a rat-killing. She'd scare off all the rats.

The Spirit of '76

Four years ago Wednesday morning, I awakened where I had fallen the night before, in an apartment on the thirtieth-some-odd floor of a high-rise apartment building in Chicago. The view was of Lincoln Park and Lake Michigan. The monthly rent was astounding.

I splashed some water on my then-bearded face and opened the front door. At my feet were two of Chicago's daily newspapers.

The message screamed across the front of both:

"IT'S CARTER!"

Thank the Lord I didn't dream it, I remember saying to myself.

Carter. Jimmy Carter. Former governor of that backward outhouse of a state, Georgia. Peanut farmer. Imagine that. Peanut farmer from Georgia running for president of the United States.

They used to ask me about him, Carter, and about Georgia. Chicagoans used to ask. "What's it really like *out there* in the South?"

"Out there" in the South. The West is "out there." The East is "over there." The North is "up here." The South is "down there." We spend millions each year to educate the heathen. And we have such vast ignorance right here in our own country.

A girl in Chicago once asked me. "Do you have any nice restaurants 'out there' in the South?"

"Surely," I answered her. "Mention my name, and maybe you'll get a good seat at the counter."

I took it all. I answered their questions. I assured them cotton wasn't growing in downtown Atlanta.

I explained we do not say, "you all," we say, "y'all," and we never use it in the singular.

I explained about grits. Unless you put some butter or cheese in them, they taste awful.

And I hurt a lot. The South was, in fact, rising again. I could read about it every day, I could hear about it on the seven o'clock news.

So why was I, a true son of the red clay whose granddaddy once owned the egg-suckingest dog in Coweta County (dog's name was Edna), stuck in Chicago?

Grizzard Buzzard luck, I supposed. Can't kill nothing. Can't find nothing dead.

I pulled as hard for him as I ever have pulled for anything, anybody. I prayed over it. "...And, Lord, if you can't help me, then at least please help Jimmy."

The night he was nominated, I couldn't hold back the tears. I ran up a hundred dollars' worth of phone calls with 404 area codes.

I got Dorsey Hill on the phone. Dorsey grew up in Rome, Georgia. "Sumbitch," he said, "don't it make you proud?"

But that was only half the battle. There was still Ford. This girl with the high-rise apartment gave an election party, and I told her I wouldn't come if any Ford people were going to be there, so we had just a small gathering (Carter lost Illinois in '76, too), but that made the victory just that much sweeter.

Four years ago Wednesday morning, I read both Chicago papers from front to back, but filled with triumph as I was, I was also never so homesick in all my life.

I think you would have had to have been away from the South to see what Jimmy Carter getting elected president in 1976 really meant to the South, and to Southerners.

I caught a cab to my office. Usually, I took a bus. I was celebrating. There was a pink memorandum slip awaiting me in my typewriter. It was from a colleague, local boy, who thought Indianapolis was the Deep South. But the man had some degree of class.

"Congratulations," began the note, "y'all ain't trash no more."

I don't know if Jimmy Carter was a good president or not, and I wish Ronald Reagan all the best.

But four years ago on a cold Chicago morning, Jimmy Carter made me as proud as if I had won the damn election myself. For that, I will always be indebted to him.

Always.

Jimmy Earl Comes Home

PLAINS—Standing here in the pouring rain Tuesday, my feet freezing, I wondered what the Ronald Reagans were doing.

Here in Plains, several thousand of us were waiting for a helicopter to drop out of the gray sky and bring Jimmy Earl home. That's what they call the former president of the United States in his hometown. They call him "Jimmy Earl."

I figured the Reagans were probably finished with their spiffy luncheon that had followed the inauguration. They were to have boneless breast of chicken and California wines.

I suppose they were probably getting ready

for Tuesday evening's inaugural ball, or maybe they were having a few pops with somebody like Frank Sinatra or Jimmy Stewart or Liz Taylor. They're all such famous friends, you know.

And while I was thinking about the Reagans, I thought about what Bill Godfrey once said. Bill Godfrey played football for the University of Georgia before Herschel Walker was born. He said, "Ain't folks nice to you when you win?"

To the winner Tuesday went the spoils. Ronald Wilson Reagan became the fortieth president. Jimmy Earl Carter Jr., the thirty-ninth, came home to Plains.

He looked awful. He looked tired and he looked drained. They said he hadn't slept in two days, as he battled to the last minute of his administration to see the hostages freed from Iran.

I think the Iranians waited, on purpose, until Reagan had been sworn in before they released the hostages. I also think the Iranians are lower than camel dung.

The crowd at Jimmy Carter's homecoming day Tuesday was vintage Georgian, vintage Deep Southern. A lady said to her husband, "Help me, Johnny, I don't think I can get my parasol open." The last person I heard refer to an umbrella as a "parasol" was my grandmother.

A woman from Macon told me, "My boss didn't want me to come over here today, but I came anyway. Jimmy Carter's the only man in the world I'd stand in the rain to see."

A little girl, sniffling, stood on the hood of a truck awaiting the former president's arrival. She held a sign that read, "We love you, Jimmy." The rain had drenched her. ABC nearly ran over CBS to get her on camera.

A sign in front of a store on the outskirts of town read, "New Rooster. Too Many Eggs. Sale. 75 Cents a Dozen. Welcome Back, Jimmy and Rosalynn."

The good ladies of Plains had wanted to turn out the world's largest covered-dish supper, and I think they did it. One table stretched an entire block, and it was filled with Southern delights, including fried chicken, and I saw bowls of collards and cakes and pies that were enough to start a riot.

They almost did. The idea was to form a line across the railroad tracks and to proceed orderly down the table, serving yourself buffet style. But several sweet-tooth vultures would not follow those directions and were pilfering from the table despite the efforts of a lady carrying a butcher knife to keep them away.

Jimmy C. Newman sang Cajun music. Tom T. Hall sang "Old Dogs and Children and Watermelon Wine." Despite the rain, the street dance and the fireworks show were still scheduled for later in the evening. I saw two old boys passing a bottle in a sack back and forth. I didn't see Billy.

When he had finally landed and had made his way to the plastic-covered platform in the middle of town, Jimmy Earl made a nice speech.

He didn't brag on himself too much. He talked about the pride he felt in having been president for four years. He said a wife of one of the hostages had said to him earlier in the day, "Mister President, I hope you can meet my husband someday." And the president replied, "I will be with him in Germany this week, and I will tell him you love him."

He asked us all to support the new president, and he talked about how much the Algerian government had helped getting the hostages released.

That started me thinking again. Here stood Jimmy Earl Carter in the middle of Plains, Sumter County, Georgia, talking about Algeria when most of us in the crowd couldn't find it on a map with directions and a head start. Nobody had come to hear about Algeria.

I got the distinct feeling that the reason that crowd showed up in that awful weather Tuesday was to help soften a hometown boy's abrupt fall from the most powerful office in the world back to private citizen. Let the Reagans dance the night away; Georgians took care of their own Tuesday afternoon.

I mentioned dancing. I will forevermore consider it appropriate that after the new president had been inaugurated, after the hostages had been freed, after dog-tired Jimmy Carter had come back to Plains and had made his speech, the last thing he did before the public eye was stand tall on the platform in front of the cheering crowd and take his wife in his arms and dance with her.

The tune was "Dixie."

Senility Test

Now that Ronald Reagan actually is going to be president, let us remind ourselves of a promise he made during the campaign.

Reagan, who will be seventy by the time he is sworn into office, promised to take a senility test if ever the situation arose where there were murmurings about the "crazy old coot over at the White House."

I think it is important that we hold Mr. Reagan to this promise. Being president is a strain on any man. Look at Jimmy Carter. He was nearly twenty years younger than Mr. Reagan when he took office. But by the time he was blown out, he was so confused, he was discussing nuclear proliferation with his daughter Amy.

You may be asking yourself what sort of senility test Mr. Reagan would take. I'm glad you asked that. Through various sources in Washington, this column has obtained a secret copy of the Official Presidential Senility Test (Republican Version).

Given after, say, two years in office, could Mr. Reagan then pass the following rigorous examination?

1. Place your hand over your heart. Would you say it is:

(a) Purring like a kitten? (10 points). (b) Humming like a Model-T Ford? (8 points). (c) Going "flap-flong-blip-bong"? (2 points). (If you are unable to answer this question because you can't locate your heart, subtract five points and do not attempt to operate an automobile.)

2. How would you describe your ability to hear?

(a) Excellent (10 points). (b) Good (6 points). (c) Fair (2 points).

3. YOU WANT THIS QUESTION REPEATED A LITTLE LOUDER?

(Subtract five points and try not to doze off during the remainder of this test.)

4. How would you describe your ability to see?

(a) Excellent (10 points). (b) Good (6 points). (c) Fair (2 points). (d) Last week at a meeting with Leonid Brezhnev you shook hands with your chair and sat down in the premier's lap. (Subtract 5 points and forget about SALT III.)

5. True (subtract 5 points) or False (add 5):

Earl Scheib does your hair.

6. Your lovely wife Nancy comes into the presidential bedroom wearing a slinky nightgown. Your first move is to:

(a) Call the kitchen and order a bottle of

champagne (10 points). (b) Look for your old Benny Goodman records (5 points). (c) Phone George Bush to see if he wants to come over and watch one of your old movies on the late show. (Subtract 6 points and say you have a sick headache.)

7. The following question has to do with your memory: Back in 1980 you won a resounding victory over your opponent in the presidential election. Your opponent's name was:

(a) Jimmy Carter. (b) Bonzo.

(If you selected (a), add 5 points to your score. If you selected (b), add 4 points. At least you were close.)

8. Another memory question: You were born in:

(a) 1492. (b) 1776. (c) 1812. (d) 1911.

(If you marked (a), (b), (c), subtract 10 points. If you marked (d), an old fellow like you should probably rest a while before we finish this test.)

9. Your youngest son, Ronnie, Jr.:

(a) Plays football for Notre Dame, like you did. (b) Is a professional wrestler. (c) Drives a truck. (d) Hops around on his toes with pale-looking girls and wears leotards.

(If you marked (a), (b), (c), subtract 5 points for wishful thinking. If you marked (d), subtract 10 points for asking your own son to never visit you in the White House until after dark.)

10. As president, your most outstanding contribution to the country has been:

(a) Getting us into a war with Canada. (b) Making Woody Hayes secretary of defense. (c) Pardoning former President Carter.

(No matter what you answered, subtract 10 points and have a glass of warm milk.)

HOW YOU SCORED

70-100: The country survived Millard Fillmore; it probably can survive you.

50-69: Get plenty of rest, avoid press conferences, and drink all your prune juice.

30-49: Move around occasionally with your eyes open. Somebody may get the wrong idea.

Less than 30: We have one chance for survival: If you do decide to push the button, maybe you won't be able to remember where they keep it.

Queen Nancy

A number of women I know never did care for Rosalynn Carter, the outgoing first lady.

"She's cold," one described Mrs. Carter.

"She wore that same horrid green dress for four years," said another.

Needless to say, these ladies are very excited now that former actress Nancy Reagan is taking over at the White House.

"She has dignity and charm," said one.

"She wears nothing but Adolfo originals," added another.

I think Nancy Reagan is a very pretty, well-dressed lady, too. But she's pushy. She reminds me of a woman who used to live in my neighborhood, Mrs. Pratt. Mrs. Pratt was pushy.

She was always offering everybody advice on how to wear their hair, what color drapes to hang in the living room, and where to hang the new picture of the bullfighter.

When you were around Mrs. Pratt, you always got the feeling she was looking down her nose at you. One day Mrs. Pratt told Mildred Elrod she was putting on a little weight. Mildred Elrod was offended and fixed it so Mrs. Pratt couldn't look down her nose at anybody again. It was too crooked after that.

I get the feeling Nancy Reagan is looking down her nose at a lot of us. She was educated at the best schools, of course, and she had spent a lot of her time lunching at expensive Hollywood restaurants, and she is great friends with a lot of rich people like Betsy Bloomingdale who go around saying, "dahling."

I first got the idea that maybe Nancy Reagan and some of her aides were snooty when one of her California cronies said, "She will bring more to the White House than Amy."

That is downright catty.

There was another remark about Nancy Reagan's style of entertaining.

"She knows how to entertain, and she'll do it with dignity, the way it should be done. There won't be anymore lemonade, cookies, bare feet, hot dogs, and Willie Nelson."

Willie Nelson, as a matter of fact, has starred in two hit movies, two more than the next president, and he rolled around in the hay with Dyan Cannon, not a monkey.

The clincher came when Nancy Reagan was reported to have said she didn't understand why the Carters didn't go ahead and move out of the White House before the January 20 inauguration so she could begin redecoration.

Jimmy Carter remains president and gets to live in the White House until the inauguration. That's according to some silly document like the Constitution, which is always getting in the way when something important like redecorating comes up.

I don't know a thing about Rosalynn Carter except what I read about her in the newspapers and what I see about her on television, but she seems a nice enough person.

She always came across as sincere. Since I wouldn't know an Adolfo from something off the bargain rack at K Mart, her dressing habits never bothered me.

She doesn't know any movie stars, I don't suppose, and she probably has never lunched on Rodeo Drive in Hollywood, and I doubt she even knows Betsy Bloomingdale, much less is friends with her, and Rosalynn talks a little funny, like folks do in South Georgia.

But she appeared to do a good job of being a wife to the president, and a mother to their children, and I would hate to see her kicked out of her house before the lease runs out.

Maybe Nancy Reagan simply needs to be reminded of something before she starts her *reign*.

Just concentrate on being a good first lady, Mrs. Reagan. A queen we don't need.

A Letter to the President

Dear President Reagan,

I purposely waited a couple of weeks before writing you because I wanted some time to think after the attempt that was made on your life. Also, I knew you were up to your ears trying to run our country from a hospital bed.

I am not pretending this will be unique, by any means, but I happen to be one American citizen who is lucky enough to have a public forum, and I see no harm in occasionally using it for expression that is purely personal.

I've got to admit up front I didn't support you in 1980. As a matter of fact, as I stood a few rows behind you as you made your nomination acceptance speech at the Republican Convention in Detroit, I said to a friend standing with me, "He sounds like he's still trying to sell a box of 20-Mule Team Borax."

My friend and I had a good laugh over that. Somehow you seemed unreal to me, too much Hollywood, not enough substance. A man nearly seventy shouldn't look as fit as you do, shouldn't bounce around like you do.

Where was your gray hair? How could you still stand so erect, speak so strongly and keep the demanding schedule those seeking public office must keep?

When you announced you would be glad to take a senility test during your term as president, I said, "Sure he will. If only he can remember where he put it."

I had some problems with your platform, too. I saw you on television night after night, smoothie that you are, telling the American people how you were going to cure inflation, bring down the unemployment rate and give the Russians hell. You *sounded* great, but I listened to a huckster at a carnival once, too, and it cost me two bucks to learn that what silver tongues preach isn't always golden.

I worried about your feelings toward the poor. I worried about what you would do the first time the Russians tried your hand. Would you react too strongly, foolishly, and get us all blown away?

I've got to admit something else, too, Mr. President. I still haven't been able to warm up toward your wife. When she suggested that the

Carters move out of the White House early so she could get to the business of redecorating, I secretly hoped her slip would show on Inauguration Day.

Your son, the one that dances, didn't impress me that much, either, especially when he called President Carter a "snake." I respected and supported President Carter, for a number of reasons:

One, I considered him to be completely honest; two, he talks a lot like I do; three, he is the only president in American history to invite me to drink beer in the back yard of the White House while listening to Willie Nelson sing. A man must have his own priorities, Mr. President.

Anyway, I've said all that to say this: I still don't know if you can pull off any of those miracles you promised, and I probably would vote for Jimmy Carter again, given the chance, but I will tell my grandchildren about the time that creep tried to gun you down in front of the Washington Hilton.

You took a slug in the lung and then walked into the hospital under your own power, cracked jokes with the doctors, went through a two-hour operation, and were signing legislation the next morning. And you're a year older than Arizona.

For right now, at least, I don't care what your politics are, I admire your vigor, your strength, and the way you handled yourself in a crisis of the utmost severity: Your own life was threatened.

Your actions said more than all the words you

have uttered as president. The citizens of this country and the rest of the world have no more doubt; At the helm of this ship of state stands the toughest old bird in the valley.

Your fan,
Lewis Grizzard

10

NUMBER ONE

I attended the University of Georgia in Athens, Georgia, from 1964 until 1968. When I arrived on campus in the fall of '64, the school's football fortunes were at an all-time low.

But the same year I arrived on campus, so did a thirty-two-year-old rookie coach named Vince Dooley. It took him seventeen years to do it, but on January 1, 1981, in New Orleans, Louisiana, Vince Dooley put a Georgia team on the carpeted floor of the Superdome that was good enough to whip Notre Dame, a team made up mostly of people from north of Greenville, South Carolina, and good enough to win the national collegiate championship.

This made me very happy. In the first piece in this chapter, I will attempt to say why. The pieces that follow will attempt to describe some of the people and places that were a part of what one quite loyal to the Red and Black described as "the second greatest story ever told . . . ."

Georgia on My Mind

I was there that first night when Vincent Joseph Dooley, who was younger then (thirty-two) than I am now (thirty-five), coached his first game from the Georgia sidelines. It was a warm September night, 1964, in Denny Stadium, Tuscaloosa. The opposition was Joe Namath and Bear Bryant's fearsome Alabama.

How I happened to be in Tuscaloosa that night is a fairly long story than can be held in check by explaining I was seventeen at the time, about to enter my freshman year at the University of Georgia. The preceding summer, I had gone to see Ed Thelenius, the Bulldogs' "golden voice," who broadcast the Georgia games on radio.

Ed Thelenius, who died in March of 1981, was nice to me and offered me a job on his

217

football crew. Ten a game and my travel and my room and my food. I would "spot" the opposition, point to the name of who had the ball for the other team. Ed Thelenius had a lot to do with getting my career started. They said he suffered a lot in the end. I hate that.

Early in the game that night in Tuscaloosa, a young defensive lineman from Georgia named George Patton stormed through the Alabama line and made a savage hit on Namath for a loss.

In the Georgia radio booth, I was sitting next to the late Bill Monday, the pioneer sportscaster who did color for Thelenius.

"They're ready!" screamed Monday. "Gawga's ready!"

Gawga wasn't ready. Namath passed them silly. The final score was 31-3. The traffic in Tuscaloosa was so bad it took three hours just to get back to Birmingham. Jim Koger, who did statistics for Thelenius, got out of the car and bought some beer. Jim Koger would teach me about a lot of things that season, including how to enjoy warm beer when there is no cold beer around. Incidentally, Jim Koger later found Jesus. There is hope for all of us.

I started classes at Georgia the next week. A lot of people, including some girls, were very impressed when I told them I worked for Ed Thelenius, who mentioned my name at the end of every broadcast.

The following Saturday, the Georgia team,

Thelenius, and I checked into the Holiday Inn in Nashville where Georgia would play Vanderbilt in the evening. Thelenius and I ate a steak. We hung around in the lobby. I remember Dooley and Georgia athletic director Joel Eaves talking together. Both seemed very nervous.

Barry Wilson, a Georgia defensive end, intercepted a Vanderbilt pass that night in Nashville, and it led to the first touchdown ever for a Vince Dooley team. The seven points was enough. Vince Dooley, head coach, and Lewis Grizzard, journalism freshman, had their first victory at Georgia, 7-0, over Vanderbilt. We would go on to be 6-3-1. We would whip Georgia Tech and we would whip Texas Tech in the Sun Bowl. Barry Wilson would later become an assistant coach at Georgia Tech.

I left Georgia in 1968. Each game the Bulldogs played while I was on campus had a special memory. I'll list a few:

—Georgia 7, Georgia Tech 0, in Athens, 1964: Driving to the game from my hometown of Moreland—I had been out of school on Thanksgiving break—a woman plowed into the back of my red 1958 Chevrolet when I stopped for gas near Watkinsville. It was her fault, but my driver's license had expired. The Oconee County policeman said he would have to take me to the courthouse, but I told him I had to be at the game to work for Ed Thelenius. He let me go.

—Georgia 18, Alabama 17, in Athens, 1965: Thelenius pounded his fist on the table in front of him after the flea-flicker play that upset the eventual national champions. It was the only time I ever saw him lose control.

—Kentucky 28, Georgia 10, in Lexington, 1965: The coldest I have ever been in my life. I knocked over coffee onto the spotter boards and all over Thelenius. He never missed a beat.

—Miami 6, Georgia 3, in Miami, 1966: I was married by now and no longer working for the football network. My wife—the first Mrs. Grizzard—and I were parked outside the Dairy Queen in Athens, listening to the game on the radio. My wife wanted to talk about something else.

"Shut up!" I suggested to her.

She dumped a strawberry milkshake on my head. We divorced the year Tech beat Dooley for the first time.

—Georgia 21, Auburn 13, in Auburn, 1966: The first Georgia game I had seen from the stands. I had worked in the press box for all the others. One of my fraternity brothers was sitting next to me in the end zone. He brought along a bottle of Jack Daniels, black. We mixed it with Coke and drank all of it. I found out Georgia had come back in the second half to win, after trailing 13-0, by reading the paper the next day.

In the summer of 1968 I went to work as a sportswriter for *The Atlanta Journal*. Those were great years. I covered a lot of Georgia games. The best one was the '71 game against Georgia Tech in Atlanta when Andy Johnson brought

Georgia back in the last minute-and-a-half to win, 28-24.

It looked bleak for Georgia that night. The Bulldogs had arrived at Grant Field with a 9-1 record, heavily favored over the Yellow Jackets. When it appeared there was no hope for Georgia, Tech sports information director Ned West walked over to Dan Magill, his counterpart at Georgia, and said, "Well, Dan, y'all have had a great season. I'm so sorry it had to end this way."

When Jimmy Poulos dived for the winning touchdown for Georgia with fourteen seconds to play, Magill walked over to West and said, "Well, Ned, y'all have had a great season. I'm so sorry it had to end this way."

In the fall of 1975, I did a stupid thing. I took the second Mrs. Grizzard and moved to Chicago to become sports editor of the *Chicago Sun-Times*. The Saturday before I began work, I drove over to South Bend, Indiana, to watch Georgia Tech play Notre Dame. Notre Dame won. I had mixed emotions about the outcome of that game.

It was very difficult for me in Chicago because I didn't care who won the Minnesota-Iowa game, or the annual battle between Northwestern and Illinois. I wouldn't walk across the street to see Michigan play Ohio State, either— two mules fighting over a turnip.

Three weeks after I had moved to Chicago, it was Thanksgiving and Georgia, with another good team, was to play Georgia Tech Thanksgiving night on national television. The second

Mrs. Grizzard had gone home to South Carolina to see her parents. I was alone.

Fine, I thought. I will purchase several cold beers, and sit back and watch Georgia play Georgia Tech. The game was to be held on Grant Field in Atlanta.

There was a problem. My neighbor across the hall in the high-rise, Near North apartment building in which I lived, had decided to be my friend. That was fine, except he was from Colombia, and I could barely understand a word he was saying. He thought I was from Zanzibar or someplace with my accent.

He invited me over for Thanksgiving dinner.

"No thanks," I said, "I want to watch Georgia and Georgia Tech on television."

"Who eeze thees Goorgea and Goorgea Tick?" he asked.

I tried to explain. His cat understood more than he did.

"You eeet, jes?" he asked again.

"No," I persisted. "I watch the game."

I cracked a beer and Georgia was scoring like mad. I think the score was 42-0 at the half. I felt wonderful. Maybe I should go have some dinner with my new Colombian friend, I said to myself.

The meal was marvelous. We switched the game on in his apartment. Tech was making a comeback.

I was feeling a bit queezy. Tech cut the final gap to 42-26. I asked if I could lie down.

"Si," said my Colombian friend. "You feel bad, jes?"

"Jes," I said.

"Probably the pot," he said.

"The what?" I asked back.

"The pot. I put eet in the dressing. You like?"

I am 800 miles away from the closest person who loves me, watching Georgia play Georgia Tech with a Colombian who has put marijuana in my Thanksgiving dressing.

I began to make immediate plans to return to Georgia.

I kept up with Georgia football while I was away, thanks to Dorsey Hill, the world's biggest Bulldog fan. Each week I would place a call to his house during the Georgia game. He would make arrangements for someone to be there who would place the receiver next to the radio.

I would sit in Chicago and listen to the Georgia games. I would do this in the privacy of my office at the *Sun-Times*. I would charge the phone call to the company. I kept watching for somebody to come and get me for doing that, but nobody ever did.

I was in Knoxville the night the 1980 season began. I was sitting next to Dorsey Hill, as a matter of fact. Dorsey never gives up. When Tennessee led, 15-0, I said, "Damn, this is a long way to come to see Georgia get beat like this."

"They're going to come back," Dorsey said. I wrote it off as the heat and the many beers working on Dorsey's head. Georgia came back to win 16-15. I would doubt him only one more time.

It was hot in Jacksonville, seven wins later, too. And Georgia had squandered so many chances to put Florida to sleep, I could feel it slipping away.

Florida scored to lead 21-20 with just minutes to play. Georgia's dream of an unbeaten season, a possible national title, were vanishing before my eyes.

"Let's get out of here," I said to the third Mrs. Grizzard.

Dorsey wouldn't budge. "I've come this far with 'em, I ain't leaving," he said.

We were in the parking lot when the third Mrs. Grizzard looked at the people on the top row of the Gator Bowl stadium and said, "Look, the Georgia fans are jumping up and down."

"Probably just a first down," I said.

"But they're still jumping up and down," my wife continued.

I noticed the Gator Bowl was shaking. I finally learned Georgia had scored on a 93-yard play to win, 26-21.

A number of people were very put out with me for leaving the stadium and giving up on Georgia that day.

"You are a disgrace," said Dorsey Hill.

Maybe I can explain. I am a terribly unlucky person. In several million hands of poker, I have never filled an inside straight nor drawn the third king.

With Georgia behind 20-21 to Florida, I reasoned the only chance Georgia had was for me to leave the stadium. With my luck, if I left the stadium, something incredible, something unforgettable, something I could tell my grandchildren about had I remained to watch, would probably happen. I left the stadium, and something did.

Georgia has me to thank for its comeback against Florida.

After Florida, Auburn fell, and then Georgia Tech, and then we all went down to New Orleans to the Sugar Bowl to play Notre Dame.

I don't know what it is about Notre Dame, but I don't like Notre Dame. I pulled hard for Jimmy Carter to win in 1976, because I was living in Chicago, and here was a man who talked like I did running for president. I pulled hard for him again in 1980 because he invited me to the back yard of the White House to drink beer and listen to Willie Nelson sing. But I pulled harder for Georgia to win against Notre Dame in the 1981 Sugar Bowl.

It meant everything to Georgia. The Bulldogs' first national championship was at stake. It meant nothing to Notre Dame save playing the role of the spoiler.

Nobody really enjoyed the 1981 Sugar Bowl game. Georgia people didn't enjoy it because it turned out to be so close, and Georgia had everything to lose. Notre Dame couldn't have enjoyed it because the Irish kept fumbling the ball all over the Superdome carpet and throwing interceptions.

I was frustrated through the entire affair. With six minutes to go in the game, when it was apparent Georgia would never get another first down if we stayed in New Orleans until Easter, I began to use abusive language.

"I can't stand you any longer," said my wife, who promptly left and went back to the hotel.

When it was finally over, tears welled in my eyes. Let me see if I can express what it meant to me and so many others.

Alabama has won national championships. So have Auburn and Tennessee and LSU. And Ohio State or Southern Cal or Texas or Notre Dame is always winning one. But never Georgia.

Georgia. It's where I was born and where my mother and father were born. We've had it rough from the start in Georgia. First we get settled by a bunch of prisoners from England. Then Sherman marches through and burns everything he can see. People call us "redneck." We finally get somebody from Georgia elected president, and nobody likes him.

But on January 1, 1981, the football team representing the University of Georgia, where I went to school, whipped Notre Dame, which gets movies made about its football teams, and won the national championship.

Grown men cried.

A friend of mine was sitting next to his fiancee in the Superdome that day. They were to be married later in the year. The wedding is off now. My friend explained:

"When I finally knew it was over, when I finally realized they couldn't beat us, when after all these years of pulling for Georgia and living with them and dying with them, I realized we had done won the by-god national title, I started crying like a baby. I couldn't stop. I looked over and there was my best friend who was at the game with me. We went to Georgia together in the sixties. We've been all over to see them play. He was crying, too. It was the most emotional moment of my life. I reached over and hugged him and kissed him square in the mouth.

"My fiancee wouldn't speak to me the rest of the day. She was mad because I hadn't kissed her first. We broke up soon after that. I just never could figure out why she thought I would have kissed her first. Hell, she went to Clemson."

Herschel Walker of Clyde's Gulf

This piece was written when Herschel Walker was driving everybody crazy by taking his sweet time about deciding which school would get his enormous talents. He did eventually sign with Georgia, of course, and he led the Bulldogs to their perfect 12-0 season, and the national championship.

Herschel Walker is a wonderful young man, incredibly talented athletically, an excellent stu-

227

dent, a polite individual who would turn down $2 million from the Canadian Football League after the 1980 season because he didn't think it was the American sort of thing to do.

Perhaps Herschel Walker isn't from Wrightsville, Georgia, at all. Maybe he's from another planet.

WRIGHTSVILLE—Football star Herschel Walker, one of the nation's most sought-after high school athletes, has ended months of speculation by announcing he is no longer planning to attend college but will remain in his hometown to work for Clyde's Friendly Gulf service station instead.

"I simply couldn't make up my mind where to go," said Walker, "so I decided the heck with all of them."

Walker had received hundreds of offers of athletic scholarships but had reportedly narrowed his choices to three schools before making his shocking announcement.

Those three schools were the University of Georgia, Georgia Tech, and Clemson, none of which were able to win him over completely.

"You ever spent any time at Clemson?" Walker asked reporters at his hastily called press conference around the self-service pumps at Clyde's. "The only excitement there is when one of the fraternities holds a tractor wash or the red light in town goes on the blink."

What about the University of Georgia? Walker was asked.

"Four years of hearing, 'How 'bout them

Dawgs!' and they would have had to mail my diploma to the funny farm," he said.

And Georgia Tech?

"Good school," Walker responded, "but I checked out who they have playing in the offensive line. Unfortunately, you can't block anybody with a slide rule. I'm afraid I'd get killed."

Walker had earlier indicated some interest in both UCLA and Southern California, but he explained they were out of the running, too.

"All they had to offer was a place to get a good suntan," Walker explained. "Now, I ask you...."

The youngster's surprise announcement was met with disbelief and amazement from coaches and supporters of the three schools Walker had reportedly been considering for his final choice.

Georgia's Vince Dooley said previous plans to rename Sanford Stadium "Walker Field" would have to be scrapped, but the Bulldog head coach said the jersey Walker would have worn at Georgia will be retired anyway.

"We spent a lot of time and effort and most of our recruiting budget on Herschel," said Dooley. "We've got to have something to show for it."

Georgia Tech's Bill Curry fainted upon hearing the news, and three hairs on his head fell out of place for the first time since he was eleven.

"Why didn't he say he was interested in mechanics?" Curry asked, upon being revived. "Some of our top graduates own their own transmission shops or Brake-O franchises. We could have set him up for life."

Clemson's Danny Ford was also stunned.

"Work in a service station? I thought the kid wanted to be with the FBI. We were flying in Efrem Zimbalist, Jr., for his first game. If he had asked, we would have even let him change the tires on the school president's pickup."

Walker bristled at questions that asked what, if any, illegal recruiting tactics had been used to attract him.

"I didn't ask for, nor did I receive, any under-the-table offers," Walker said. "One school did offer me my own private dorm and a summer job as a bank president, but that is quite legitimate.

"I simply looked at what was available to me, and the decision to stay home and work for Clyde seemed the best. Besides, he's giving me Wednesday afternoons off and an employee discount on tires and tune-ups."

"He starts to work Monday morning," said a beaming Clyde. "I don't expect him to learn everything overnight, but the kid's gonna be a great one."

Big Night in ObKnoxville

Dorsey Hill, the world's biggest Bulldog fan, still hasn't gone back to work.

"I declared Monday 'Herschel Walker Day' in the state of Georgia," said Dorsey, "and, of course, nobody with red and black in his heart would work on 'Herschel Walker Day.'

"Tuesday, I was too hung over from 'Herschel Walker Day' to work. I'm going back Wednesday to open my mail, and then I have to take Thursday and Friday off to get ready for Texas A&M."

I've mentioned Dorsey in this space many times before. He graduated from the University of Georgia in 1966. He drove a 1957 Chevrolet convertible and was one of the first inductees into Bubber's Hall of Fame.

For those who received their higher educations elsewhere, Bubber's is a package store in downtown Athens which is steeped in tradition.

Dorsey would walk into Bubber's on a Thursday night, buy eight bottles of Red Hurricane wine (ninety-seven cents a bottle) and disappear for days.

Enough background. Dorsey's excitement this week is appropriate, of course, after Georgia opened its 1980 season with a 16-15 victory over Tennessee Saturday night in Knoxville.

"It ain't 'Knoxville,'" Dorsey always reminds me. "It's 'ObKnoxville.'"

Dorsey has no love for those of the Volunteer persuasion.

I attended the game myself and can now boast of having been a part of the largest crowd ever to gather for a sporting event this side of Ann Arbor, Michigan.

At last count there were 95,228 of us, bunched together in the sweltering heat. Several hundred were reportedly still sober when the game kicked off.

Quite frankly, I got sick and tired of the Herschel Walker recruiting story. I heard so much about where Herschel Walker, an eighteen-year-old, would attend college I secretly hoped he would stay home in Wrightsville and work for Clyde's Gulf.

But I must admit that after watching his performance in ObKnoxville Saturday night, he is apparently worth all the trouble, and whatever else, that it took for Georgia to ink him to a pact, one of my favorite sports cliches.

Have you ever watched a kid's game of football where one kid was so much better than all the other kids you felt sort of sorry for all the other kids?

Herschel Walker looked like that Saturday night. Clearly, he was the best athlete on the field, and my favorite part of the game was where he ran over the safety from Tennessee and the poor youngster didn't move for several moments.

"He won't be able to run over people in the Southeastern Conference like he did in high school," the smart money was saying only a few weeks back. Give him the ball and he could run over the Russian infantry.

Anyway, it was a marvelous experience, and since I was able to get a seat on a chartered bus, I didn't have to endure any of the traffic problems which are the rule around Neyland Stadium and the infamous local highway system affectionately known as "Malfunction Junction."

I also picked up one other Dorsey Hill gem I must share:

When Dorsey Hill goes to a football game, he makes a full-scale tour of it. Dorsey left Atlanta four days before kickoff and drove around the entire state of Tennessee to, as he put it, "get a feel for the game."

"Did you learn anything from your tour?" I asked Dorsey.

"Sure did," he replied. "I learned the three most overrated things in this world are extra-marital sex, home cooking, and Rock City."

God Is a Bulldog

JACKSONVILLE, FLA.—Dorsey Hill, the world's biggest Bulldog fan, left here Sunday afternoon, bound for Auburn, Alabama, where Georgia's undefeated football team next appears.

"I don't think you can get from Jacksonville to Auburn," I had said to him.

"You change buses in Waycross and Columbus," Dorsey answered.

"You aren't going home first?"

"Home?" He screamed back. "I haven't worked since Texas A&M, and I haven't slept since Clemson. You expect me to go back home when we play Auburn in only six more days?"

I lost my head, I suppose.

A lot of people lost their heads here Saturday afternoon. Georgia played Florida. Georgia won the game, 26-21. It's a lot more complicated than that, however.

Georgia came into the game ranked second in the nation. To continue to compete for its first Big Banana ever, the national championship, Georgia had to continue its winning streak.

Florida ("bunch of swamp lizards and beach bums," according to Dorsey Hill), wanted to step on the Georgia dream.

Dorsey arrived here Thursday afternoon with thousands of others who made the early departure south from various points in Georgia. Many of those individuals were drunk as five-eyed owls by the time they reached the Florida line.

As local wit Rex Edmondson says, the Georgia-Florida game is the "annual celebration of the repeal of prohibition."

Dorsey waited until Friday to get into his serious pre-game drinking, however.

"I stopped at the New Perry Hotel Thursday for lunch and filled up on collards," he said. "It's hard to drink on a belly full of collards."

Agreed.

Now that I have had time to digest all that did eventually happen in college football Saturday, I think I can say without fear of charges of blasphemy that the whole thing was a religious experience.

"Deacon Dan" Magill, the "Baptist Bulldog,"

read a prayer Saturday morning to the Georgia faithful in which he beseeched the Almighty to help the Bulldogs "smite the Florida Philistines."

Then, there was the game itself. Georgia behind 21-20, ninety-three yards away, time running out.

"We need a miracle!" screamed Dorsey Hill, now fortified with more than collards.

Georgia got its miracle. Buck Belue to Lindsay Scott, for ninety-three yards and the winning touchdown with only seconds remaining.

If that wasn't enough, there was the astounding news from Atlanta. Georgia Tech had tied No. 1 Notre Dame. Surely, Georgia will be ranked first in America when the ratings are released.

"A tie was a gift from heaven," said Dorsey. "Notre Dame gets knocked out of number one, but Tech doesn't get a win. God is a Bulldog."

Verily.

I must make one confession here. I did it, and I must suffer the consequences.

I gave up at Jacksonville Saturday afternoon. Florida had the ball. Florida had the lead. There was only three minutes to play. I left the stadium. I was in the street when the miracle came.

"You are a gutless disgrace," Dorsey Hill said to me later.

He detailed my punishment:

"We're going to a tattoo parlor in this very town tonight," he began. "And you're going to have '26' tattooed on one of your cheeks in red. And you're going to have '21' tattooed in black on the other cheek. I don't want you to forget what you did."

I won't, but which cheeks is between me and the tattooist.

Charlie Harris

We're talking about thirty years ago. Sanford Stadium on the University of Georgia campus didn't have those double decks and seated maybe half of what it does today.

The players wore those funny-looking helmets, with no face guards, and they wore those awful high-top shoes Johnny Unitas would never give up.

Herschel Walker hadn't been born. Vince Dooley, the Georgia coach, was just a kid player himself.

Korea was happening.

That wonderful year, 1950. That was the year Charlie Harris arrived in Athens to play football for Georgia. Wally Butts was the head coach. Hard times—compared to the '40s and to the present Georgia season—had set in.

But halfback Charlie Harris would help Butts and the Bulldogs pull themselves together again, so the theory went.

He was fast. He was quick. He was, in the day before the term was used, a "franchise," a 1950s version of Herschel Walker, if you will.

He came in from a place called Goodwater, Alabama. Before he would leave, Dan Magill would nickname him, for his fleet moves, "The Gliding Ghost of Goodwater."

Charlie Harris had an excellent career at Georgia. He never reached the heights of a Trippi, a Sinkwich, a Tarkenton, nor, of course, a Walker, but he had his moments. He even captained the track team.

His four Georgia seasons were to be spread out in seven, however. After the '50 season he went into the Marine Corps and put in three years on the Camp Pendleton team.

"We had a lot of people trying awful hard to make that team," he remembered.

Get cut, get sent to Korea. That's pressure.

Charlie Harris came back to Athens after the Marines, played on the 1954-55-56 teams, had a cup of coffee with the Cleveland Browns, and later gave it a brief shot with the New York Titans, forefathers of the Jets, in the first season of the American Football League.

After that, Charlie Harris became a high school football coach, and that is where I met him. He turned up at Newman High School at the same time I was John Q. Student. He taught my health class, where you learn not to brush your teeth the way everybody brushes their teeth.

But enough of history. I thought about Charlie Harris all day Saturday. Herschel Walker of Georgia was breaking all-time NCAA freshmen rushing records. Mike Kelley of Georgia Tech was drilling passes.

Thousands were cheering. And Charlie Harris lay in his bed fighting a dog called leukemia.

It happened last April. Look at Charlie Harris. He's what they call a physical specimen. Still a long-distance runner at forty-nine.

"I was a runner before it became popular to run," he says. "Twenty miles was nothing for me."

The original marathon man. Never drank. Never smoked. Shamrock High principal. Husband. Father. Church man.

"I hadn't been to the doctor in twenty-three years," Charlie Harris said.

But in April, his endurance went. The ten-mile runs became six-mile runs, and then four-mile runs, and then, "I really didn't know what to do. I played under Wally Butts, and I guess I learned it there. You run everything out. Suddenly, I couldn't run it out anymore."

Leukemia was diagnosed. It got worse, then better. Lately, it has gotten worse again.

Charlie Harris and I talked the other day. I owed him at least a telephone call. Besides trying to save my teeth, he did me another favor seventeen years ago.

We talked about the chemotherapy, and the possibility of a bone marrow transplant, and I said the usual stupid things, like "Get well soon" and "If there's anything I can do. . . ."

And Charlie Harris said, "What you learn from all this is nobody is indestructible."

Nobody, the man said. Not even the Gliding Ghost of Goodwater.

The lesson is there for the taking.

Charlie Harris died in the spring of 1981.

Mrs. Walker

WRIGHTSVILLE—The way you get to Herschel Walker's house from "downtown" Wrightsville, county seat of Johnson, is you take a right on Idylwild Street and then you drive halfway back to Dublin looking for a white house on a hill across the railroad tracks.

You miss the house three or four times. When you finally sight it, you cross the tracks and drive up a dirt road to the small frame house where Herschel lived until he departed for Athens and the University of Georgia and fame and what will likely amount to a fortune before he quits carrying footballs.

Outside the house, dogs appear from nowhere. Two little dogs, and one big dog who is a dead ringer for the dog that hung around Spanky and his gang.

"That's Herschel's dog," says one of Herschel's brothers, who has emerged from within the house. "That car (a red '55 Chevy) is Herschel's car, too." That car turns out to be Herschel's "second" car. His main wheels roll under a Pontiac Trans-Am.

Inside the house is the Herschel Walker Trophy Room. Plaques cover the walls, trophies stand on every available surface. In the middle of it all, strangely, hangs a frame that surrounds the faces of Robert and John Kennedy and Dr. Martin Luther King, Jr.

The house is ten degrees past being warm. It is neat and warm. It is filled this evening with children and grandchildren, and I notice that Herschel Walker's family's television is black and white.

In a few years, when Herschel turns professional, he can buy his family color televisions. Wall-to-wall.

I am here to see Herschel Walker's mother because nobody knows Herschel Walker any better than she does. It has occurred to me there could be somebody from another planet reading this who doesn't know who Herschel Walker is.

Briefly, he's the best college football player alive. He plays for the University of Georgia. He's just a freshman, and you can watch him Thursday when he and his team meet Notre Dame in the Sugar Bowl.

Christine Walker, the good wife of Willis Walker, works all day in a local clothing factory. She is a small, pretty woman with a soft, reassuring voice. God gives mothers voices like that for a reason.

We talked in her living room. She sat on one end of the couch, me on the other.

I asked her how much Herschel weighed when he was born. He is the fifth of seven children.

"Eight pounds and three ounces," she answered. I noticed her face break into a momentary beam. Mothers do that when they remember when their children were babies.

I wanted to know what he ate when he was growing up.

"Peas," said Christine Walker.

"Peas?"

"That boy loved peas," she went on.

I asked what kind of peas.

"Red-hull peas," she said. "That's all he wanted to eat until he got a little older. Then he started eating hamburgers. I worry about him getting a balanced diet because all he wants is hamburgers."

Herschel Walker doesn't eat a balanced diet.

And he weighs 230 pounds and he runs like the wind. Put that in your blender and drink it.

I asked Herschel's mother if she ever spanked him.

"When he didn't mind," she answered.

I asked her what advice she gave Herschel when he left for college.

"I told him to make sure he leaves some time for his academics. I always stressed academics to him, and he paid attention to that. He always wanted to learn."

I asked her if she were proud of her son.

"Lord, yes," she answered, and there was that beam on her face again.

One other thing I asked her. I asked her if there was ever a time she was against her baby boy playing football.

"I tried to talk him out of it in the eighth grade," she said.

"Why?" I asked.

"I was afraid he might hurt somebody."

Magill

In the university town of Athens, Georgia, there was a pub called Harry's. Not really a pub. Outside of Atlanta, pubs are beer joints. And they served the beer cold and in cans at Harry's, with pickled eggs and a meaty tasty called a "Slim-Jim."

Later on autumn evenings in a simpler time that was the early sixties, the Slim-Jims were a nickel and there would be an inevitable gathering inside and around one of Harry's wooden booths. The crowd—five, six, sometimes seven or eight—would include an assortment of individuals who had as bonds a daily thirst for the canned brew, at least a fringe involvement with University of Georgia sports, and, perhaps most of all, a love for the spun yarn. Some of the stories told there over the years were true.

The floor was open for the first couple of

rounds. The silver-haired English professor would recite his dirty limericks again: "There was a coed from Fitzgerald..." began everybody's favorite. A sportswriter from Atlanta had a rumor: Dodd at rival Georgia Tech would soon retire. An ex-Georgia football player who never left town or graduated would insist again that the coaches of the time cussed less on the practice field than they had in his day. "Three years after I played out my eligibility," he would begin again, "I still thought my name was 'Pissant.'"

Soon, however, the chirping of the sparrows would cease. And, as it always seemed the good Lord had intended, the man of every evening hour at Harry's, one Daniel Hamilton Magill, would assume verbal command to speak at great length and with never-ending embellishment of tales that rivaled those of the deaths of kings.

I was a nineteenish sports editor of the local morning journal at the time, no more than tolerated by Harry's regulars. Nearly two decades later there has still been no manner of man to compare with, the Lord-bless-him, Magill.

Magill is a genuine, living legend, although that may not be apparent at first glance. He is balding. He laughs at his own jokes, and he turns red in the face. He is married to a Phi Beta Kappa and could have been one himself. He did as well in school as he did, he says, because he sat next to "A-plus Mason" and "Straight-A Milligan." He has three children. Two are girls, both former beauty queens. His son was a top tennis player at Princeton and is now a heart specialist.

Magill, and it is always simply "Magill," may be further introduced in a number of ways. He was Georgia's director of sports information for thirty years before being named assistant director, as well as director of athletic department public relations. Magill is fifty-eight. He is the University of Georgia tennis coach, and has been since 1955. Magill is also a long-play album on Georgia sporting history, and he has worked seven days a week, week in and week out, at it. All of this may be more commendable than epic, but I have entertained a two-decade-old notion that this man's life was destined for cinematic exposure.

But consider if one were casting a movie of his life and times. One would need, say, a Charlton Heston for Magill's own tennis prowess that continues full-throttle on a senior level. One would need an Ozzie Nelson for Magill's campus stereotype, and a taller George Gobel, in his comedic prime, for the Magill wit. And then go out and find somebody like Will Rogers for tale-bearing qualities.

And remember, too, that here you are dealing with one of the greatest Deep South accents since man drawled the first "y'all." Tex Ritter had a fair-to-middling Southern accent. Charles Laughton, of all people, as Senator Seab Cooley of South Carolina in *Advise and Consent*, was

Hollywood's best attempt. But in Magill, you have South-in-the-mouth that is matchless.

Such are the problems that arise when the task is to capture Magill in the limits of the printed word. The beauty of one of his stories, one of his lines, can be mocked by a chosen few. But arriving at a suitable re-creation armed only with a typewriter makes coming close all that is achievable.

Suffice it to say, Magill's "great" is not "grate," but "greyette." His "coach" is more "co-atch."

It is only with the preceding rambling characterization and the subsequent apologetic groundruling that Magill may be tackled further. What follows knows no order, either. To pull order to Magill would be nearly disrespectful. Offered next is simply Magillobilia that goes in a thousand different directions, trying to keep up:

Magill grew up in Athens and has been a nonresident only twice: once as a Marine officer in World War II and another time as editor of high school sports at *The Atlanta Journal* in the late forties. His father was editor of the *Athens Banner-Herald*, and, at fourteen, the son became sports editor. He was paid two movie passes a week.

It was during these formative years that Magill took his first step toward a lifetime as a matchless promoter. He had taken a dual interest in snakes and tennis and he saw no reason why the two could not be combined for fun and profit.

Magill had served his snake apprenticeship

under Ross Allen, who went on to become snake-handler supreme in Florida. Allen had worked at the Athens YMCA camp and young Magill was one of his students.

Soon afterwards, it fell upon Magill to become caretaker of the University of Georgia tennis courts, honest-to-goodness red clay that they were in those days. Magill chose the courts as the logical site for his first great promotion, a Depression-days snake fight between his own Casper Kingsnake and Rastus Rattler, who had been captured in the north Georgia hills and transported to Athens via bicycle by one of Magill's friends.

A capacity crowd was on hand at a dime a head. "The crowd," Magill can still remember and recount with his special flair, "became so large and noisy it frightened the combatants. Neither Casper nor Rastus would move from their appointed corners. It was touch-and-go for several moments."

The promoter saved the farm, however. Magill's stick-prodding of Rastus brought a strike from the prodee, and Magill's leap in retreat satisfied the customers.

"I don't really know what happened," he was to say years later. "But we finally put my Casper and Rastus in the same cage together after it became apparent they were not inclined to fight. I returned to check on them several days later, and only Casper remained in the cage. There was a rather satisfied look upon his face, and he seemed to have gained a few pounds.

*   *   *

Magill later promoted successful high school all-star games in Atlanta while working for *The Atlanta Journal*. He put together a Jack Kramer-Bobby Riggs tennis match in Atlanta in the forties and drew more than 3,000, the largest tennis crowd ever in the South at the time. His Georgia tennis matches have often drawn larger audiences than Georgia basketball games in the massive, 10,000-seat Coliseum. Incidentally, attendance figures at Georgia athletic contests are official: Magill, with a quick glance to the stands, estimates them.

As sports information director, Magill had the responsibility of handing out press box tickets, compiling miles of statistics, and publicizing Georgia athletics. What wasn't a duty, but is now a tradition, is Magill's conjuring the alliterative nicknames for Georgia Bulldogs athletes. There have been some classics:

Bobby Walden, who went on to punt for the Pittsburgh Steelers, was Magill's "Big Toe from Cairo." (Keep in mind that the south Georgia city of Cairo is pronounced "Kay-ro.")

Kicker Spike Jones was "Sputnik Spike."

Savannah running back Julian Smiley was the "Chatham Cheetah."

Halfback Charlie Harris was known as the "Gliding Ghost of Goodwater, Alabama."

Fullback Ronnie Jenkins, a south Georgian, had a couple of Magill nicknames. Magill called him "The Wild Bull of the Flatlands" for his running ability.

"He was a great blocker, too, on the Georgia championship team of 1966," Magill remembered. "He used to literally knock people out with his blocks. I called him the 'Ebullient Embalmer' because he always smiled at his opponent before cracking him. He really enjoyed his work."

Quarterback Andy Johnson, now with the New England Patriots, was Andy "The Unimpeachable" Johnson to Magill. Perhaps Magill's greatest accomplishment, however, was the nickname for German-born placekicker Peter Rajecki, known as the "Bootin' Teuton."

The 1980 season brought Georgia its brilliant freshman running back, Herschel Walker, and Magill reportedly went into seculsion in his back yard vineyard for hours before coming out with "the best I can do right now," that being "Herschel the Unmerciful."

Magill gives credit to one of his understudies in Bulldoggerel, Dewey Benefield of Sea Island, for what he considers an even better nickname for Walker. It was a Benefield poem that followed Walker's debut against Tennessee that referred to the Wrightsville Wonder (my feeble attempt) as "That Goal-Line Stalker, Herschel Walker."

(It's even bettah when you heah Magill pronounce it: "That Goal-Line *Stawlkah*, Herschel *Wawlkah*.")

It was in tennis that Magill's rhyming nirvana

may have been reached. It was during the NCAA finals in Athens that the Flouri brothers of Missouri showed up as a doubles act. Long after they had been ousted from the tournament, Magill still delighted in calling them from the press box's public address system: "Will 'Flooorey' and 'Flooorey' from 'Mizooorey' please report...."

Magill has frequently even been called on by the university to perform duties of great importance. It was Magill who took upon himself the burden of finding a new tennis coach for the university in 1955.

"Several turned me down," he recalls. "So finally, I decided I would take the job myself." Later, so the story goes, it was suggested to Magill that Georgia had been lucky he had appointed himself to the tennis position. "Indeed" was his reply.

Indeed, indeed. Magill has built a tennis dynasty at Georgia. His teams have won the Southeastern Conference tennis championship nine of the last eleven years. His 1981 team finished third nationally. Magill was honored in 1980 at the U.S. Open Championships in New York for having recorded his 500th victory as a collegiate tennis coach.

Magill was himself a tennis player and varsity swimmer at Georgia. He has a string of state and Southern singles and doubles tennis titles and still plays every day. It is table tennis at which he may be most adept, however.

He won the state singles championships ten of the twelve times he competed from 1933 to 1958. He also played what legend records as the longest single point in the history of the game, a point he eventually lost. Magill and his opponent were hooked up in a match at the Athens YMCA. In walked an innocent bystander who inquired as to the score: "Three-two, Magill" was the reply. That information in hand, off went the bystander uptown to a movie. He returned to the YMCA some hours later, following a double feature, and was surprised to see the match still in progress. Again he inquired as to the score. Again came the reply. "Three-two, Magill."

There are those who insist that there should be a special Magill Practical Joke Hall of Fame. Two of the incidents that belong there are as follows:

Once Magill was returning with his tennis team from a match in Tallahassee, Florida. The team, traveling in two cars, stopped for gas in Thomasville.

"How do we pay for this, Coach Magill?" asked the player who was driving the car that pulled to the pump first.

"Just tell the man I'll take care of it, and you go on ahead after you have filled up," Magill, in the rear car, answered.

The player did what Magill told him and drove off. After filling Magill's car, the attendant asked Magill to pay for the gasoline he had pumped into the first car.

"Pay for what?" Magill asked. "I've never seen those people in that car before in my life."

Legend has it that it was in Dublin where the authorities finally caught up with the victims of Magill's joke. (They were released in time to win the next match.)

Magill once had a secretary who was the perfect subject for one of his famous telephone tricks. The secretary had arranged a party—complete with champagne—for a Georgia basketball coach who had just completed the school's first winning season since the Roosevelt administration—Teddy's. In the Georgia governor's house at the time was Lester Maddox, a teetotaller who wanted everybody else to be.

Magill answered a rigged call, ostensibly from Atlanta and the state capitol.

"Well, Governor, I don't think the girls have meant any harm with having a little champagne at the party even though this is a state-supported institution," he began. The secretary was aghast. The argument got hotter. Magill ended it with, "Well, to hell with you, too, you little ballheaded bigot!" The secretary, swear those who were there, fainted.

Magill has other accomplishments touching lightly on the near-athletic.

He has, for a long time, claimed the title of world's fastest two-finger typist. He was once challenged by a journalism professor, who typed full fingered. Could Magill's two outdo the professor's ten? Final score: Magill, fourteen lines; journalism professor, twelve.

Magill also claimed the world's two-fingers-only chinup title as well. He would perform on any available half-in door facing. Tragically, he was challenged one day at lunch after a tuna sandwich.

"My hands were greasy, and I slipped off," Magill contends. A broken collarbone was the result.

Magill refers to himself as a "chain soft drink-drinker." He has his own soft-drink machine, which was presented to him by the Athens Coca-Cola Company and is decked with a plaque that bears his name. His addiction to soft drinks is such that there are those who say that in the days he scored Georgia baseball games, he connected a garden hose from the press box to the men's room directly below for nature's calls at mid-inning.

There is no Georgia fan as dedicated to the cause as Magill. There is no Georgia fan who is any more foursquare against the "enemy," rival Georgia Tech, than Magill.

He contends that Georgia Tech's Grant Field has a slightly higher seating capacity than Georgia's Sanford Stadium because the Grant Field seats are smaller. One must thus be a "squint-ass" to enjoy a Yellow Jacket game. Georgia victories and Tech losses on same Saturdays are praised as "doubleheader sweeps."

Perhaps no voice in history has ever spoken with more bias or with more pure love than when Dan Magill speaks of his University of Georgia. Breathes there a Bulldog with soul so dead that he doesn't respond emotionally to the standard beginning line of every Magill speech:

"My fellow Georgia Bulldogs, chosen people of the Western world."

Doug Barfield

Auburn University, Vince Dooley's alma mater, attempted to hire him away from Georgia after the 1980 regular season. In all the shouting and anxious moments concerning Dooley's decision— which was eventually to remain at Georgia—the forgotten man was the man Auburn fired in order to make room for Dooley. Doug Barfield. Major college football is a cruel, unforgiving sport that can cast you aside on the whims of fools.

Before the Vince Dooley-Auburn thing is put to rest completely, I wanted to bring up one more name.

Doug Barfield.

I've never met Doug Barfield. Frankly, I wouldn't know him if he walked into my office and asked me to dance. But I have this thing about underdogs, and Doug Barfield qualifies as one. In spades.

He was Auburn's football coach until Monday. He spent a total of nine years at Auburn University, five as an assistant coach and the last four as the head coach.

He never had a chance. Seldom, if you follow a legend, do you have a chance, especially in the fickle arena of sports.

Doug Barfield followed the beloved Shug Jordan as Auburn's football coach and it was just a matter of time before the alumni ax fell upon him.

The same thing happened to Bud Carson, who followed Bobby Dodd at Georgia Tech, and to countless others. The man who follows Vince Dooley at the University of Georgia will probably just be marking time until he is canned.

I don't know if Doug Barfield was a good football coach or not, but the only measure these days seems to be: Did you win all your games? A negative answer to that question can have you in the insurance business overnight.

Pepper Rodgers, who got fired as Georgia Tech's head football coach because the alumni didn't like his hair, said to me once: "Coaching is the craziest business in the world. If you're a brain surgeon and your patient dies, you can walk out to the family, look sincere, and say, 'I'm sorry, but I did all I could do.' And you still get paid.

"In coaching, some nineteen-year-old drops

the football and you lose the game, and they'll run you out of town."

They were talking big bucks in the will-Dooley-go-to-Auburn crisis. I read $1.8 million. Imagine that. And here was Dooley struggling with the decision:

Do I stay in my beautiful home in Athens and make all this money here, or do I move into a beautiful home in Auburn and make all that money there?

The human side of this story is, what in the devil was Doug Barfield doing all that time?

Auburn has been his home for nine years. He has two children enrolled at Auburn.

"He was torn asunder by all this," an Auburn man told me Thursday.

I remember back several weeks ago when the rumors started flying that Barfield would be fired. A man named Charles Smith, a member of the Auburn Board of Trustees, made all sorts of noise about finding a coach who would be tougher on the players than Barfield.

Charles Smith runs a laundry in Montgomery. Can you imagine having some guy who runs a laundry deciding how well you were performing in your chosen profession?

More on Doug Barfield from my friend in Auburn:

"He's warm. He has more class than he's ever been given credit for. He's kind. And under all this pressure and criticism, he was a man of steel."

While Auburn officials offered Dooley the farm this week, Doug Barfield quietly resigned. He said, "I don't want to be anyplace I'm not wanted." He also said, "But I don't feel like I have to hide my face."

I wouldn't be a football coach if you gave me the pick of the cheerleaders.

Monday, when all the hoopla about Dooley was at its height, Doug Barfield was in Montgomery. He had been summoned for federal court jury duty.

Each prospective juror was asked to stand before the court and give his name, place of residence, and occupation.

Doug Barfield stood and said:

"Doug Barfield.

"Auburn, Alabama.

"Unemployed."

War Eagle.

This One Is Forever

NEW ORLEANS—I am writing this from the sixteenth floor of the Howard Johnson Motor Hotel in downtown New Orleans. I can see the top of the Louisiana Superdome from this perch. It looks more like one of those ominous nuclear power plants than a sports stadium. The truth is, the place exploded, what is now four hours ago.

I am no stranger to madness. I have attended an Indianapolis 500 automobile race, the annual salute to mental illness. That was nothing compared to this.

This was wild. This was crazy. This was downright scary at times.

A cop on the floor of the Dome said, "Thank God they ain't armed."

A security man screamed to no one in particular, "I've got the damn president of the United States in here and I can't get him out!"

A female member of the Notre Dame band, holding onto her flute as she surveyed the incredible scene before her, said, "If it meant that much, I'm glad Georgia won."

It meant that much. Grown men cried. A man kissed Georgia defensive coach Erskine Russell squarely on the top of his bald head. Erk just smiled.

I saw a man get down on his fours and bark like a wild dog (dawg) and try to bite passersby. A woman I had never seen before lifted her skirt to show me her underpants. "Georgia" was stitched hip to hip.

Let me take you back to when the playing of the 1981 Sugar Bowl Football game between Georgia and Notre Dame first began to show signs of the subsequent emotional explosion that it became.

New Year's Eve on Bourbon Street. It's the Red Sea. If there are Notre Dame people in town, where are they?

The 1 Bourbon Street Inn, in the very heart of the French Quarter, is packed with Georgians. The third floor balcony is Bulldog Central. The bathtubs in the adjoining rooms are filled with ice and champagne.

The people in the street, thousands of them, scream, "HERSCHEL!"

The people on the balcony respond, "WALKER!"

A chant aimed at what brave or stupid Notre Damers might be in earshot begins:

"YOU GOT THE HUNCHBACK! WE GOT THE TAILBACK!"

"The Pope's a dope" came out a couple of times, too—there's one in every madhouse.

At midnight there was much kissing and hugging and how-'bout-them-dawging and speaking of dogs (dawgs), the Georgia mascot, "Uga," showed up at the party on the third floor Bourbon Street Inn balcony, and I heard one man say to another:

"Hey, how'd your lip get cut?"

To which the second man replied. "I was kissing 'Uga' on the mouth at midnight and he bit me."

When the sun rose on 1981, there were those still partying from the night before. Three hours before kickoff, the city was covered in red. Red hats, red pants, red shirts—red. I was to discover later, underwear as well.

The Game. So close. God bless Mrs. Walker. Thirty seconds are left, Georgia leading, 17-10.

Notre Dame can't stop the clock. At :14 show-
ing, the game ends because every Bulldog from
Rabun Gap to Tybee Light and Hartwell to
Bainbridge has charged onto the floor of the
Louisiana Superdome.

They trampled each other. They trampled
the players, the coaches, the press, they ripped
down a goal post.

The public-address announcer pleaded and
pleaded and pleaded: "Please clear the field!
PLEASE clear the field!" They turned off the
lights, but the Georgia band kept playing, and
the people, that delirious mass of people, kept
on celebrating.

It got ugly a couple of times. Secret Service
men trying to get Jimmy Carter out of the
building shoved a few citizens around.

And then there was this group of little girls,
the "High Steppers" from Shreveport or someplace, who had competed for the right to perform at the Sugar Bowl. They were cute little
girls wearing cowboy hats. They were left out of
the pregame show because the teams stayed on
the field too long. They were promised they
could perform after the game. They lined up,
all neat and nice, but there was no way.

One little girl said. "I don't want to go out
there. We might get hurt." They finally gave it
up and went back to Shreveport. Sad.

But it was also bright and beautiful and bois-
terous and an All-American sort of thing that
other schools have enjoyed, so now it is Geor-

gia's turn to point that finger to the sky. It may be days before the last Bulldog leaves New Orleans. The streets would not be safe Thursday night.

Number One, by God. Number Ever-Lovin'-One. The sign in the Georgia locker room had said it all:

"This one is forever."

11

PEACH STATE

I was born in Fort Benning, Georgia, in the wee, morning hours of October 20, 1946. As an adult, I have left Georgia to live in another place only once. For nearly two years, I was a prisoner of war in Chicago, Illinois, a cold place where it often gets dark at half past four in the afternoon.

Georgia is a diverse state, with spectacular mountains and a sun-splashed seacoast and piney woods and rolling fields and Atlanta, a city in a park. I love the state like I would a good woman. I revel in her beauty and charm, and I forgive her every fault.

I love the way her people act and think and talk. I love her Macons, her Savannahs, and especially her tiny Snellvilles. I love her good ol' girls who will still cook a man a homemade biscuit in the morning, and I love her good ol' boys who weren't bothering anybody, and then Billy Carter's brother went and got himself elected president.

There was that country song, "If I Ever Get Back to Georgia, I'm Gonna Nail My Feet to the Ground." I did. And I have . . . .

Shove It Up My What?

I received an angry note the other day from a Ms. Gloria Schmaltz, who used to live in Atlanta. Now she lives in Portland, Maine.

Believe it or not, I have been to Portland, Maine. It is a seacoast town, a little dingy as I recall, but lobster was cheap.

Ms. Schmaltz's note was brief, but there could be little question as to what had raised her ire.

Me.

It seems some of Ms. Schmaltz's former friends in Atlanta had sent her one of my old columns that concerned what I consider to be a major issue—homemade biscuits.

Ms. Schmaltz read the column and then wrote me the note.

"Reading it," began her message, "helped me remember why, at age thirty, I retired to the

North. It is good old boys like you that bring out my hairy-legged worst."

Then, Ms. Schmaltz really got nasty.

"You can take your South," she wrote, "and shove your biscuits up your Confederarse."

Pretty talk, Ms. Schmaltz.

I really feel terrible about all this. Here a woman has moved all the way from Atlanta to the dingy little seacoast town of Portland, Maine, just to get away from the strain of Southern male we know as the "good ol' boy."

Shucks, Ms. Schmaltz, was it something we might have said? Was your mother frightened by a pickup truck while she was carrying you?

Perhaps you were offended by our music, Willie and Waylon and Merle and Conway. Sorry, we just like to pat our foot occasionally and hear a song or two about cheatin' and hurtin' and old dogs and children and watermelon wine.

I've got it. You think we drink too much. I guess we do, but a good ol' boy's longneck beer is sort of his security blanket, like if somebody insults the good name of Richard Petty, you are secure in the knowledge you are holding onto something you can break over his head.

We're loud, maybe? I guess we are, but we're colorful. Know how many good ol' boys it takes to screw in a lightbulb, Ms. Schmaltz?

Four. One to screw in the lightbulb, one to write a song about it, and two more to start a fistfight in the parking lot.

And then there's football. You probably don't care a thing about football, do you, Ms. Schmaltz? Good ol' boys do, of course, and that probably bothers you.

But give us that, Ms. Schmaltz. A fellow has to have something to hold his interest when he's not fishing or playing with his dog.

And that column I wrote about biscuits really bothered you, didn't it? You have to understand I wrote it as a public service.

Do you realize the divorce rate in this country? All I did was quote the great philosopher Jerry Clower, who is of the opinion that if more women would cook homemade biscuits for their husbands in the mornings—instead of serving those horrible impostors that come from cans—the divorce rate would go down.

I also wrote that women who wouldn't cook homemade biscuits occasionally probably wouldn't shave their legs, either.

That was just a little joke, Ms. Schmaltz, but I noticed in your note you mentioned something about being "hairy-legged" yourself. That certainly doesn't make you a bad person, but in the words of my boyhood friend and idol, Weyman C. Wannamaker, Jr., a great American, "I wouldn't take a hairy-legged woman to a rat-killin'."

All I am saying, Ms. Schmaltz, is don't judge us too harshly, and please try to understand that good ol' boys need love and understanding, too.

Incidentally, since your heart obviously wasn't

in the South you left, I, for one, am glad you got YOUR Confederarse out.

Of Giggling Yankee Girls

I made a 300-mile automobile trip recently, and I noticed the summer's wanderlust has brought out the hitchhikers in great numbers.

I still offer an occasional lift to a hitchhiker, despite the fact that next to "Always wear clean underwear, you might be in a wreck," my mother's favorite piece of advice was, "Never pick up a hitchhiker."

But how can I resist? In my youth I rode my thumb to all sorts of wondrous places, like once all the way from my hometown in Moreland, Georgia, to Daytona Beach, Florida, and back.

I never spent more than two hours at any one stretch without a ride, and a carload of Yankee girls picked me up just outside Palatka and took me the rest of the way into Daytona.

To a Georgia country boy of sixteen, getting to ride in the same car with a group of Yankee girls is a rare and, as I was to discover later, valuable experience.

"Talk for us," they would plead, and I would say things like "yawl" and "dawg" and "grey-its," and they would giggle and talk about how cute I was.

Many years later, standing uncomfortably alone

at a bar on the east side of New York City, I recalled that experience, and in a loud voice, began to say "yawl" and "dawg" and "grey-its." Soon I was surrounded by a gaggle of giggling Yankee girls talking about how cute I was.

It doesn't take much to impress Yankee girls, bless their hearts.

The surprising thing about the hitchhikers I saw on my trip was they all looked rather unkempt.

I even saw a young man hitchhiking with no shirt. He obviously was a rookie. There are certain rules every hitchhiker should know, and the first one is: Never try to catch a ride looking like you've just escaped from reform school.

When I was hitchhiking, I always tried to portray the right-young-man-probably-trying-to-get-to-his-grandparents'-house-for-a-visit image.

You don't need a coat and tie for that, but neat clothing and a recent haircut are important, not to mention a look of sincerity about you that will assure the driver trying to decide whether to pick you up that you likely remain after Sunday School for the worship hour and you don't make a habit of cutting throats.

Also, it is important to remember: Once you have gotten a ride, to keep your mouth shut. Let me explain why:

A friend and I were hitchhiking together. My friend was from a very religious family. We caught a ride with a man and his wife.

A few minutes after we had been picked up,

the man lit a cigarette. My friend said to him from the back seat, "Please put out that cigarette."

The man said, "Why, kid?"

And my friend said, "Because if the Lord had intended you to smoke, he would have given you a smokestack, that's why."

The man pulled over and put us out of his car. It was the middle of the night somewhere near Eastaboga, Alabama.

"If the Lord had intended you to roll," the man said, "he'd have put wheels on your butts."

We spent the remainder of the night in a cornfield. Big-mouth stayed awake and prayed for a ride that never came. I slept. And dreamt of giggling Yankee girls.

How to Spell "N-e-k-k-i-d"

A picky reader wrote recently to protest the way I often choose to spell the word that means not having any clothes on.

The dictionary way that word should be spelled is "n-a-k-e-d." Sometimes it is okay to spell it that way. Most of the time, however, I prefer to spell that word "n-e-k-k-i-d."

There most certainly is a difference. "Naked" does, in fact, mean having no clothes on. "Nekkid," on the other hand, means not having any clothes on and you're up to something.

For example:

"We all come into this world *naked*."

But, "Let's get *nekkid* and run through the woods."

My point here is that a writer, especially one from Georgia, should not have to be chained to the formal spelling of a word when another spelling and pronunciation conjures a better image of what the writer is trying to portray.

Take the word "police." That does just dandy when you type something like, "Police in Toledo today announced the arrest of. . . ."

But that doesn't work when you want to type, "Why are all the police in Bogalusa so fat?"

In that case, the word must be changed to "poh-lice," as in "Joe Billy hit Marvin on the head with a beer bottle and then Darlene called the *poh-lice*."

I hope this is making sense. Regardless, let's go onward, and, as long as we're in the area of law enforcement, consider the words "motorcycle" and "siren."

I prefer "motor-sickle" and "sireen," as in, "The *poh-lice* were chasing Joe Billy on their *motor-sickles* and their dang-blasted *si-reens* were loud enough to wake the dead."

A colleague and I were discussing this very same matter recently, and he brought up the problem of "threw" and "through."

"If you say, 'He *threw* something *through* something,' it sounds sort of weird," my colleague explained.

And how do you get around such a problem?

Simple. By the use of one of my favorite words, "thowed," as in "He *thowed* something *through* something."

I could go on all day:

● "Business": That is fine unless you are describing a Southern male involved in the selling and trading of previously owned automobiles. Then, he is in the used car *bidness*.

● "Ask": There is no such word south of Louisville, Kentucky. The word is *ast*.

● "Sucker": Sometimes that works. Most of the time, *suckah* seems to say it so much better.

Let's end this with a simple exercise: Using the new spellings you have learned for the words mentioned above, make up a cute little story. Okay:

"Joe Billy and Darlene of Bogalusa had a thing going on, but one day Joe Billy caught Darlene and Marvin running *nekkid* through the woods. Joe Billy chased down Marvin and *thowed* him through the bushes and then hit him up side the head with a beer bottle.

"Darlene called the *poh-lice*, and here they come on their *motor-sickles* with their *si-reens* turned up loud enough to wake the dead.

"The *poh-lice* caught Joe Billy and hauled him off to jail. Marvin had fourteen stiches and missed two weeks off from his used car *bidness*.

"Darlene, meanwhile, ran off with Harvey, another poor *suckah* who's *astin'* for trouble."

Snellville: Part I

My father was born in Snellville, Georgia, in a house on a hill that now stands above the Thriftown store off highway 78. When he was a young man, he was in the retail hot dog business here. "I ran a wienie joint," is how he described it.

"One day these two old girls in a '36 Essex coup lost control of their car and ran all up in my little wienie joint," he'd laugh.

Was there any damage?

"Was there any damage? There wasn't an onion left, son. Not an onion."

I went out to my father's grave Saturday afternoon. We brought him home when he died and buried him next to Adolphus and Eugenia, his parents. The cemetery sits in a corner of a pastureland across the road from Zoar Methodist Church, out a ways from town.

I don't really know why people go and stand over graves. It's been seven years. But it was peaceful out there Saturday. Black Angus cattle were grazing to the right, and I hadn't seen that in a while.

Zoar church was established in 1811. It's frame and painted white and probably hasn't changed that much in all this time. They've added on to the back, it looked like, and there may be air conditioning now. That spoiled the memory of a favorite scene—the women fanning themselves on hot Sunday mornings with those fans Zack Cravey used to hand out when he was running for Georgia fire commissioner again.

Snellville is maybe twenty miles from downtown Atlanta. It used to be no more than one of those proverbial bumps in the road to Athens.

You take the Stone Mountain freeway and then two-lane 78 east to get there. Traffic can be tough. Snellville has graduated into a full-fledged bedroom community of Atlanta. Population is 7,000 and growing.

There is a housing development called Lake Lucerne in the area. Lake Lucerne is formerly Possum Pond. Snellville cometh of age. But its pace is more sensible. I was assured the drugstore still serves Coke as God intended: Two squirts of syrup and a dash of carbonated water.

Snellville gave itself a "day" Saturday. There was a parade, of course. Senator Sam Nunn was the grand marshall. It's not an election year, so there were no long speeches.

There was a Jaycee barbecue. Six hundred-fifty chickens went to heaven, and you could have all the iced tea you could drink. The Monroe Girls Drum and Bugle Corps hasn't missed a parade since Moby Dick was a minnow. They were there. Gordon Tanner and the Junior Skillet Lickers danced, the Matthews Family Gospel Group sang about Jesus, and a Marine band played "God Bless America" while the old men stood at attention.

That evening they had a baseball game. I went with Ludlow Porch of WRNG radio, Snellville's most celebrated citizen. We sat in the Bermuda grass along the rightfield line and fought off the mosquitoes. "Only one thing worse than mosquitoes," Ludlow said, "and that's running barefooted through the pasture and stubbing your toe on a stob."

Snellville's South Gwinnett High played Gainesville. The game was tight. Both managers chewed Red Man and spat a lot. I caught the Gainesville signs. Right hand across the letters and two spits for steal.

The score stood 1-1 in the middle innings when a South Gwinnett batter fouled a couple off behind the screen into a corn patch and then lined a pitch over the centerfield fence into what we used to call a pine thicket; 2-1. In the same inning, another South Gwinnett batter homered to right. The South Gwinnett pitcher, a youth called "Bonut," as in "donut," held off a Gainesville rally in the last inning, and the Snellville team won the game, 3-1.

They build all those big stadiums and pay out all that money. It was here I saw a sixteen-year-old shortstop go deep into the hole, stab the ball, turn completely around and throw the runner out by a half step.

Both teams met in the middle of the field when the game ended and congratulated each other. Admission was free.

Afterwards, there was a street dance up at the Thriftown parking lot.

"I've been everywhere there is to go, and I've done everything there is to do," the old man used to say. "I probably should have never left Snellville."

I used to wonder what he meant by that.

Snellville: Part II

The startling success of "Dallas," CBS' prime-time soap opera, has the other two networks searching feverishly for something to rival the giant hit.

"We don't want a carbon copy of 'Dallas,'" a source at NBC said, "But we do want a program that would offer the same week-to-week suspense."

"Exactly," echoed a high-ranking executive at ABC. "Networks have copied each other for too long. We want our own 'Dallas,' but not really a 'Dallas,' if you know what I mean."

I love that big-time television talk.

I was going to hold back on this for a few more months, but with all the hoopla "Dallas" got over the weekend for finally revealing who plugged J.R., I suppose I should go ahead and release the news:

Yours truly is busy at work on a script for a new television prime-time soap opera that he will sell to the highest bidder, who may then blow "Dallas" halfway to El Paso.

Get the picture. The camera pans the horizon, and then the triumphant name is spread across the screen:

"SNELLVILLE"!

Yes, television fans, "Snellville," the dramatic new series that follows the lives and loves and trials and tribulations of the Gooch family of Snellville, Georgia, bedroom community to the booming metropolis of Atlanta.

You want strong characters, I'll give you strong characters.

Meet Billy Oscar (B.O.) Gooch, the tyrannical eldest son of Grover (Big Tuna) Gooch, who founded the powerful Gooch Fish Market, "Your Channel Catfish and Mullet Headquarters in Snellville and Gwinnett County since 1913."

Then, there is B.O.'s mama, Big Tuna's wife, Pigella (Miss Piggie) Gooch, who can scale and clean a mess of bream in two shakes of a cow's tail.

Which brings up Sophie Jo Gooch, B.O.'s wife, who wasn't bad looking until she got hooked on twinkies, and now she's the size of the county dump truck.

One day a man was passing through Snellville and saw Sophie Jo standing in front of the fish market.

He walked inside, and B.O. asked if he would like to order a mess of channel cat, fresh from nearby Possum Pond.

"No," said the man, looking out the window at Sophie Jo, "but what'll you take for your whale?"

Also in the script is Wanda Jo, Sophie Jo's dynamite little sister who comes to visit the Gooches for the summer. And then there is B.O.'s younger brother, Norbert (Oyster Face) Gooch, and his wife, Carmelita, whom he met when she came through town doing a motorcycle act for the carnival.

The immediate family also includes Darlene Gooch, precious granddaughter, whose parents deserted her for the nightlife and brights lights of Loganville.

Here's the plot: You put all these people in the same double-wide mobile home at the Bide-A-Wee Trailer park, and the possibilities are endless.

B.O. is fooling around with Sophie Jo's sister, Wanda Jo. Sophie Jo, meanwhile, is just sitting there feeding her face another batch of Twinkies.

B.O. is also trying to run his brother, Oyster Face, out of the family fish business at the same time Oyster Face's wife, Carmelita, is laid up with three broken ribs and a cracked head from trying to drive her motorcycle up the steep side of Stone Mountain.

B.O. is a no-good creep whose clothes always smell like fish. The only friends he has are local cats who always follow him when he walks down the street.

The plot thickens when, in the last episode of the season, B.O. is beaten senseless with a frozen bass by an unnamed assailant.

Who shot J.R.? Who cares? Who belted B.O. with a frozen bass?

"SNELLVILLE"! It even smells like a hit.

The Sweetwater Inn Open

It was something out of a dream urbanites with rural roots probably still have occasionally if they haven't forgotten what home was like.

Saturday afternoon in a small town. It is hotter than the law should allow. Fat folks, old folks, and dogs seek the shade. Nothing is moving with any semblance of speed save the Southern Railway freights that roll through town on their way to the yards in Atlanta.

A number of wise men had gathered at the Sweetwater Inn in Austell—maybe twenty miles from downtown Atlanta out I-20. I can't describe the Sweetwater Inn in any other fashion. It is a beer joint, classic in both appearance and clientele. I mean no disrespect. I hold beer joints dearer than most. I did my undergraduate sin in one.

The juke box is mostly Conway and Loretta and Waylon and Willie. They got a dime for a Tampa Nugget but only eight cents for a King Edward Imperial. A chopped barbecue sandwich is seventy. Sliced is eighty. A longneck Bud is fifty-five. The beer is moving ten-to-one better than anything else on this day.

Inside the conversation ranges from politics to sports to inevitable fishing lies. A man swore he caught 508 catfish out of Sweetwater Creek. Another man cast doubt. It was too hot to take the disagreement any further.

Outside they were pitching horseshoes. A couple of times every year, Don Mitchell—who owns the Sweetwater Inn—gives a tournament. This was doubles only. The Sweetwater Inn Open Horseshoe Tournament. Open because they came not only from Austell, but also from Powder Springs, Mableton, and even Conley. Trophies are the prizes.

From what I could gather, the horseshoe pits in the pine grove out behind the Inn used to be the Forest Hills of horseshoe pitching in Georgia. Once, state tournaments were even held there. But a few years back, pitching on a state level sort of galloped away and now Don Mitchell just gives his own tournaments and the boys get together for the frolic they provide.

A relic of a grander day is still in evidence, however. Underneath the vines and brush that border one side of the pit area, a sign, bearing the names of former state horseshoe champions, has fallen in rust and apparent neglect.

During the tournament Saturday, one of the contestants—several longnecks into the afternoon—relieved himself upon the sign. Other sports send their grand masters to halls of fame and cast statues in their likenesses. Old horseshoe pitchers, it would see, are not as fortunate.

The game is to fifty. The tournament is double elimination. Ringers count three. Leaners, one. Any deviation from that scoring system is immediately put down. "Barnyard horseshoes," they call it. Some pitchers throw a flop. There are also three-quarter and one-and-a-quarter throws, depending upon the number of revolutions the shoe makes en route to the stob. A competition horseshoe weighs two-and-a-quarter pounds. Don Mitchell gave another tournament a few weeks ago on Austell Day and calculated that three tons of horseshoes went back and forth between the stobs.

The action had been underway a couple of hours by the time I got there. Only three teams were left. Wayne and his partner Mack already has a loss. Gene and Paul had not been beaten and neither had Don and Bud. They were to meet head-on.

There were fifteen in the audience. Fourteen watched from wooden benches. One stationed himself under a pine tree to the rear of the pitchers. It was there he eventually gave in to the beer and the sun, and it was there he missed the Sweetwater Inn Open Horseshoe Tournament as he slept the sleep of the innocent.

Gene wore Bermuda shorts in the showdown match and went to his truck before the first pitch for something to help in the heat. Paul stuck to the beer. By a prior commitment to each other, Bud and Don weren't drinking. Don, said Bud, had been saved recently.

279

Paul was off from the very start, and Bud and Don jumped to an early lead. Two sets of double ringers off Bud's low, accurate flop throw put his team over the top. Paul and Gene then met Wayne and Mack in the losers' bracket. Wayne is the Frank Tanana of Austell horseshoe pitchers. He and Mack moved into the finals and took Bud and Don twice—50-42 in the final game—for the championship. Wayne threw twenty-eight ringers and three sets of doubles in that final.

I asked him his secret. I think he was serious. "Don't get too drunk," he said. Don't let them put your name on that sign, either, Wayne.

You forget things like this can still happen, that places like this still exist. I had a good time. So did another spectator who had just moved into Austell from Miami. He sat there with a chew in one side of his mouth and a cigar in the other. He drank his beer in long gulps.

At one point he walked over to me and said, "All I need now is a scarlet woman."

"How's that?" I responded.

"I've got everything else," he said. "I'm chewin', I'm smokin', I'm drinkin', and, dammit, I'm cussin'."

We drank a toast to the good times.

Billy

I guess we should have known the Billy Carter story was not going to have a particularly happy ending when we saw him posing for a picture wearing a hat made out of pop-top rings from beer cans.

You may or may not remember that picture, but I do, and I remember thinking at the time I saw it that a man in full control of himself and his destiny likely would not pose for such a picture.

America needed Billy Carter back when he burst through the screen door of the nation's consciousness, grinning that boyish grin of his and pulling on a can of PBR, back in 1975.

We were just getting over stuffy old Nixon and all sorts of other disasters, and here was some redneck galoot who said what he thought, got drunk when he pleased, and would wear no man's necktie, no matter that his high-hatted brother was trying to be the president.

So, the nation took to Billy Carter for a time, like a child takes to a new bauble, and Billy Carter responded to the call by going around doing weird things like posing for the picture with the pop-top hat.

Everybody wanted to drink a beer with Billy Carter in those days. Including me. I found my way to Billy's service station in Plains one afternoon with this good ol' boy from Chicago who was down for a visit, and we must have drunk half a case each, and finally I had enough to ask Billy if he'd pose for a picture with me and my friend.

Billy would have posed for a picture with a snake in those days if somebody would have held its head still. My friend took the picture back to Chicago and showed it around and was a mild celebrity himself for having mixed in such company.

I don't think Billy Carter ever intended to do anything wrong. He simply got caught playing a game in which he didn't understand the rules. Good ol' boys from Plains and other rural outposts know they've done wrong when they spend a night in jail, get fired from their jobs, cuss in front of the preacher's wife, or run their trucks in a ditch.

Making insensitive remarks about this group of people or that group of people or taking silver saddles from this nation or that nation, or relieving yourself under the sky when nature calls, isn't anything to give a second thought about.

But Billy Carter's brother happened to be president, so when the booze got to Billy, and the business deals started to get heavy, and the Libyans started to court him, and instead of being "cute" he was now "tacky," the nation reacted in the typical American way. It dropped Billy Carter like a hot potato.

I was reading the latest about him the other day. The IRS is on his tail for $100,000 in taxes owed.

"They're out to get me," Billy said.

And they'll get him. The IRS always gets its man.

Rosalynn Carter said the other day that Jimmy is doing just fine in his role as ex-president. He'll write a book, of course, and make a lot of speeches, and, in his spare time, there's always his woodworking.

I suppose Miss Lillian will continue to get along, and sister Ruth has her career and sister Gloria still is playing harmonica, I suppose.

Meanwhile, Billy is still trying to make a living and keep the IRS wolves away from his door, and he's not even supposed to have a drink anymore. I wonder if he's still able to muster that boyish grin.

Historians will identify further the legacy of the Carter administration, but already I can name at least one of its unsuspecting victims: brother Billy, who would have been better off if he'd just waited outside in the truck while Jimmy went in to be president.

Moon Over Moreland

MORELAND—This was home for a long time. The lady responsible for me has been sick, but there was still enough left from gardens past to put a gracious plenty on the supper table. We sat up until well past ten. The main topic of conversation was the standard warning from the lady that too many cocktail parties can clear a path to destruction. She's right, you know.

Moreland is in Coweta County, forty miles southwest of Atlanta. The last census said 300 people live here. There are no traffic lights. There are two churches. One is white frame. The other is red brick. They sink you in one. They sprinkle you in the other.

Some of the better memories relate to sport. The Baptist Church sponsored a baseball team. I was a Methodist nine months of the year. Summers, I sang a different ecclesiastical tune for obvious reasons.

We played the games on the field behind the grammar school. It doubled as a rock pile. Anything hit on the ground was an automatic lethal object. Somebody had to stand deep behind the batter's box to save foul balls from being lost in a sea of kudzu and milkweed. An even greater danger was a foul ball landing in a bird dog pen past the weed patch. Bird dogs won't normally bite, but they will chew a baseball beyond recognition and further use in a New York minute.

I won't mention his name because he might still be in reading distance, but the funniest thing that ever happened was an overweight teammate swinging mightily at a pitch, missing it, and splitting his tight-fitting uniform pants in the rear.

In his haste to make the game on time, he had neglected to wear underdrawers. Moon over

Moreland. The game was halted a half-hour while he streaked home to have his mother repair the damage. He never lived it down, of course, but the child also never left home again without one snug pair covering his boobango and a spare in his pocket in the event of another such emergency.

We never heard of tennis or golf. Never *heard tell* of tennis or golf, as went the native tongue. Basketball was an outdoor game. Football was choosing-sides touch in the lot across from the Methodist Church.

The street was one goal line. A sapling was the other. My cousin, a great receiver, went long toward the sapling end of the field. As he turned to take in the pass, he caught the tree flush at full stroke. A brilliant career ended at the same moment. So did prayer meeting, just beginning inside the church, when they heard what my cousin called that sapling after he came to.

I drove around for nostalgia's sake after the lady's breakfast the other day. Even Moreland has changed here and there.

Where we played touch football stands an edifice the county has erected. "That sonufabitchin' saplin" was gone. I smiled at what might have been my cousin's avowed revenge against it. There are even a couple of tennis courts where I remember a cornfield. Wonders never cease. The old baseball field has lights now and a screen to stop foul balls. I suppose those bird dogs went to their last hunt and chewed the stitches out of their last Reach Official a long time ago, anyway.

I walked out into the dew that covered centerfield. Little Eddie played centerfield. There was the day I was pitching. We led 3-2, or maybe 5-4. It was late in the game, and the other team had runners on. I grooved one and the batter hit a shot to deep center. How can I still recall that sinking feeling? How can I still recall Little Eddie, without a prayer, running a full gait, chasing after what would surely fall to the red clay earth and roll halfway to Luthersville?

A few months after that Little Eddie was dead. The car went out of control, and he was thrown from his seat. He couldn't have been more than fourteen. His folks took it hard. It tore the town apart.

He caught the ball. Little Eddie ran and he dived and, by some grace, he caught the ball.

A Little Piece of Heaven

Except for the time my mother and I were following around the man who gave me this name and the couple of years I was held prisoner of war in Chicago, the splendid state of Georgia has been home.

I love the south. I have few good memories

that did not come from within its bounds. I especially love Georgia.

I am a product of its public schools. I attended its state university, just like Herschel Walker, the football player, does now.

I love the incredible diversity of this state, the largest state east of the Mississippi River. (That will win you some bar bets.)

Georgia has miles of beautiful coastline, but the mountains of North Georgia have an even stronger hold upon me. I can lose myself for weeks among them. And Georgia has the massive, piney flatlands of its broad southern bottom, and it has spectacular, cosmopolitan Atlanta, and it has hundreds of crossroad towns like Hahira and Split Silk and Roosterville and Primrose, where they talk and move slowly, praise the Lord on Sunday mornings, and generally are made of the good, strong stuff that holds a society together.

It hasn't been easy for Georgia. I moved to Chicago in 1975. In 1975, people in Chicago would ask me, "Are there any nice restaurants 'out there' in Georgia?"

I did my best.

"Georgia," I pointed out, "is 'down there.' Omaha is 'out there.' And there are a couple of nice places to eat. Mention my name and maybe you'll get a good stool at the counter."

We've been called "rednecks" and worse. We've been terribly misunderstood. Chicago remains a hotbed of racial contempt, but I was chided during my sentence there for the unfair, stereotype vision of hooded Klansmen walking every street from Rabun Gap to Tybee Light.

H. L. Mencken once described Georgia, and the South, as an "intellectual Gobi." H. L. Mencken made that observation from the lovely city of Baltimore.

But we had our moment in the sun, Georgia and Georgians did. Tucked away in a little corner of the country, the rest of the nation discovered us four years ago, and we enjoyed a brief flirtation with celebrity status.

Suddenly, in Chicago's Division Street bars, my drawl was an object of great interest.

"Say something Southern," they would demand.

"Sumbitch," I would answer. They would howl.

A Chicago friend wanted to try grits. I invited him to my apartment for a Deep South breakfast. Along with the grits, the menu included country ham, red-eye gravy, and biscuits.

As the breakfast was being prepared, the friend walked into my kitchen, took one look at the biscuit dough and said, "So, that's grits?"

How we lost the war remains a mystery to me.

Jimmy Carter brought us out of our relative obscurity. He was our governor, and then he ran for president in 1976 and got himself elected.

I was just sitting here thinking: It all comes to an end Tuesday. Ronald Reagan will become the new president. Jimmy Carter will return home. Georgia will be out. California will be in.

I received a Christmas card with "Jimmy and

Rosalynn" stamped on the bottom a few weeks ago. I framed it. A man is lucky to make one presidential Christmas card mailing list in his lifetime. I don't look to do it again.

There probably will be a period of adjustment for us. No more network commentators broadcasting from downtown Plains, no more "Georgia mafia," and Billy Carter gives way to a smart-mouth son who wears very tight pants.

But we will adjust. We always do. And what will be left in the place of all that attention of the four previous years will be what was here all along.

A little piece of heaven, just south of Chattanooga.

Y'all come see us. You heah?

__ BOOK OF STUPID QUESTIONS
(V38-972, $7.95, U.S.A.) (V38-973, $4.95, Canada)
An irreverent, hilarious parody of the *Book of Questions* with topics ranging from the merely ridiculous to the truly pointless.

__ OTHERWISE ENGAGED
(V38-702, $6.95, U.S.A.) (V38-703, $8.95, Canada)
A hilarious tongue-in-cheek guide to the trials and tribulations that every newly betrothed couple must conquer to achieve wedded bliss.

__ DADDY COOL
(V38-584, $6.95, U.S.A.) (V38-585, $8.95, Canada)
A hilarious guide for fathers that shows them how to be cool, in spite of being a dad.

339